Topics in Autism

Demystifying Autism Spectrum Disorders

A Guide to Diagnosis for Parents and Professionals

Carolyn Thorwarth Bruey, Psy.D.

Sandra L. Harris, Ph.D., *series editor*

Woodbine House ◆ 2004

All rights reserved under International and Pan-American copyright conventions. Published in the United States of America by Woodbine House, Inc., 6510 Bells Mill Rd., Bethesda, MD 20817. 800-843-7323. **www.woodbinehouse.com**

Excerpts from the *Diagnostic and Statistical Manual of Mental Disorders*, Fourth Edition, copyright 1994 American Psychiatric Association on pages 52-60; 64-68; 71, 72; 76-78 were reprinted with permission.

Library of Congress Cataloging-in-Publication Data

Bruey, Carolyn Thorwarth.
  Demystifying autism spectrum disorders : a guide to diagnosis for parents and professionals / By Carolyn Thorwarth Bruey.
       p. cm. — (Topics in autism)
  Includes bibliographical references and index.
  ISBN 1-890627-34-8 (pbk.)
  1. Autism in children—Diagnosis—Popular works. I. Title. II. Series.
  RJ506.A9B78 2004   618.92
  618.92'89—dc22   DRU
                            5.06
                                                            2004001185

Manufactured in the United States of America

10 9 8 7 6 5 4 3 2 1

For Dr. Sandra Harris
Mentor, role model, and friend

TABLE OF CONTENTS

1 | Introduction

The Potter Family

Clark and Mary Potter are in shock as they leave the clinic. Their son, Sam, has just been diagnosed with an "autism spectrum disorder." Although the Potters suspected that their three-year-old son's development was a bit unusual, the possibility of autism never crossed their minds.

Their only knowledge of autism comes from Hollywood and made-for-television movies that depict these children as excessively remote and uncommunicative. But this image does not fit their little Sam, who laughs uproariously when tickled and enjoys chasing his older sister Lily around the house. They had noticed Sam's speech was delayed and that he showed some "quirky" behaviors; however, they had attributed these behaviors and delays to the fact that they had not paid as much attention to him as they had to Lily, when she was a young child.

Did this lack of attention "cause" Sam to have an autism spectrum disorder? What do the doctors mean when they say Sam has an "autism spectrum disorder"? Is it the same as "autism" or a different diagnosis altogether? When they look for information at the library and on the Internet, the Potters feel overwhelmed with all the jargon and apparently contradictory advice. Their family and friends, although supportive, are little help in providing answers to their many questions.

The Kennedy Family

Nancy and Bill Kennedy are the proud parents of five boisterous children. They had both wished for many children and enjoyed the inherent chaos of a household of offspring. They welcomed the birth of their youngest child, Kelly, and anticipated her integration into their busy family life. However, it was soon apparent that Kelly's development was unusual. Early developmental milestones such as walking and talking were delayed. By the time she was three years old, comprehensive testing indicated that Kelly, in fact, had mental retardation and would require specialized education. Although the Kennedys were understandably concerned about their daughter's future, they vowed that Kelly would receive every support possible to help her reach her potential.

As time passed, Kelly progressed slowly but surely within the special education system. However, professionals started to wonder if Kelly was experiencing more than just mental retardation. In addition to her obvious delays, Kelly showed some unusual behaviors, such as flapping her hands in front of her eyes, staring at bright lights, and becoming very upset if there were changes in her routine. Although Kelly responded relatively well to adults, she rarely played with her siblings or classmates When she was seven years old, Kelly's pediatrician concluded that she had autism as well as mental retardation. Bill and Nancy questioned this diagnosis. Their perception was that children with autism were exceptionally bright. How could Kelly have both autism and mental retardation? If, in fact, both diagnoses were accurate, which one should drive her education and overall treatment?

The Potters' and Kennedys' stories are not unusual. Many parents like the Potters, with no prior knowledge of autism spectrum disorders, find themselves desperately researching the field in an attempt to better understand their child's needs. The task can be overwhelming, exhausting, and frustrating. As with the Kennedys, parents of older children may be faced with changing opinions regarding their child's diagnosis. After having finally adjusted as best they can to one particular diagnosis, they now have to readjust their thinking and may begin to question the professionals' decisions. As described in Chapter Six, determining which autism spectrum disorder, if any, is the appropriate diagnosis for your child can be a very confusing process. Parents often get caught up in a whirlwind of questions and concerns.

How Will This Book Help Me?

This book aims to help parents and professionals in the field of autism spectrum disorders better understand the diagnostic process as well as gain a broader knowledge of autism spectrum disorders in general. The information included in this book will be particularly helpful to parents, including those whose children have not yet been diagnosed but are questioning the possibility of an autism spectrum disorder, as well as those parents whose children have already been diagnosed within the spectrum. You will gain a fuller understanding of the ways that the various autism spectrum disorders are assessed, the part that you and professionals play in this evaluation process, what to do if you question the diagnosis your child has received, emotional reactions you may experience, what treatment strategies may be helpful, and resources that may help.

Why is This Book Needed?

Historically, the prevalence of autism was cited as approximately 4 to 5 per 10,000 births (Wing, Yeates, Brierly, & Gould, 1976). However, the reported incidence of autism spectrum disorders has increased significantly over the past decade and current statistics indicate that as many as 1 in every 500 children fall within the spectrum (Croen, Grether, Hoogstrate, and Selvin, 2002). The field of autism spectrum disorders is in the midst of ever-evolving definitions and treatment strategies that can be highly confusing to those of us caught up in the whirlwind. As a consequence, like the families described earlier in this chapter, more and more parents are finding it necessary to become experts in a field that had previously been unfamiliar to them. Although there are a wide variety of books and other resources available, very few address the finer points of differentiating the five diagnoses within the autism spectrum. In addition, few guide parents who are beginning to suspect their child may fall within this diagnostic category.

Before getting down to the nitty-gritty of autism spectrum disorders, we should clarify a few points. Traditionally, children with autism were said to have a "pervasive developmental disorder," or PDD, for short. This phrase implies that a child demonstrates a *disordered* development (i.e., peaks and valleys in skills) that has a *pervasive*, or significant, effect on the child's overall abilities. As described below and in further detail in Chapter Four, five separate subcategories of pervasive developmental disorders have been identified. More recently, the phrase pervasive developmental disorders, or PDD, has been replaced by the expression "autism spectrum disorders." Since "autism" is a more widely acknowledged term, incorporating this word into the diagnostic description is meant to decrease confusion.

> Thirty years ago, the incidence of autism was reported to be 4 to 5 per 10,000 people. Today, its prevalence is estimated at 1 in every 500 people.

Although many people in the general population are familiar with the term "autism," most are less familiar with the term "autism spectrum disorder" or with the names of its five subcategories. As a consequence, parents and many professionals tend to rely upon using the term "autistic" when describing any child whose development falls within the spectrum. Such global labeling has resulted in much confusion, and this issue will be discussed more fully in Chapters Four and Six.

Over the years, it has become more apparent that the behaviors, skills, and potential exhibited by children with autism spectrum disorders vary greatly. Whereas one child may show very slow progress and eventually require notable supervision for the rest of his life, another child may demonstrate greater success and become an adult living on his own with minimal assistance. The image of a spectrum, or continuum, allows parents and professionals to recognize this wide range in skills and behaviors.

For the purpose of this book, the more contemporary phrase "autism spectrum disorder," or ASD, will be used as a synonym for the more traditional phrase pervasive developmental disorder. The terms autism spectrum disorder and ASD will be used interchangeably throughout this book as umbrella terms for the five subcategories of syndromes included within the spectrum. These diagnoses are:

1. autistic disorder,
2. Asperger's disorder,
3. childhood disintegrative disorder (CDD),
4. Rett's disorder, and
5. pervasive developmental disorder-not otherwise specified (PDD-NOS).

Why is it Important to Diagnose Children Who Have an Autism Spectrum Disorder?

Some parents and professionals think labeling a child limits a full understanding of the whole child by merely categorizing them into a designated group. After all, a child with an autism spectrum disorder is a child first and foremost. No one will debate that children with autism spectrum disorders show a wide range of abilities and personalities. If parents and professionals treat all children labeled as having an ASD in the same way, individualized education and treatment will be nonexistent.

So, we recognize that merely labeling a child does little to promote improvements in his development. **But,** there are many compelling reasons to determine whether or not the diagnosis of an autism spectrum disorder fits your child. The following is a list of reasons a definitive diagnosis will benefit you and your child in the long term.

- Knowledge is power! As parents, a diagnosis gives you a better understanding of your child's needs.
- Diagnosis leads to appropriate treatment. A label of autism spectrum disorder is your child's key to appropriate specialized services in educational settings as well as in the community. Without documentation of diagnosis, your child will very likely miss out on crucial learning opportunities.
- Research studies have repeatedly shown that early diagnosis of ASDs can make a significant difference in terms of a child's eventual prognosis. Although an early diagnosis is optimal, a diagnosis at any age can open the doors to effective treatments that might otherwise be overlooked.
- Parents frequently cite feeling validated when told that their child has an autism spectrum disorder because they feel their concerns had been discounted in the past.
- Getting a diagnosis will help you get connected to other parents who will be an ongoing source of support.
- Merely having a label can sometimes be helpful when explaining your child's development to siblings, other family members, people in the community, etc. By noting that your child has "autism," others will have a better understanding of your child rather than misinterpreting his behaviors.
- Many funding streams and treatment resources are available only if a child has a specific diagnosis.

Many studies have shown that appropriate treatment for children with ASDs under five years of age can greatly increase the chances they will progress and eventually be included in regular education classes. A few studies have even indicated that some children who are diagnosed at a very young age, then provided intensive teaching methods, can enter typical kindergarten classes and require no more special education support for the rest of their lives.

Confusion and Potential Misdiagnosis

Given these positive research results, why is there still considerable hesitancy and confusion when determining whether or not a child has an autism spectrum disorder? One of the major drawbacks to clear and consistent diagnoses within the ASDs is that the diagnoses are purely *behaviorally based*. That is, as of today, there are no medical tests such as blood work, genetic work-ups, EEGs, etc., that can definitively determine whether or not a diagnosis is warranted. Therefore, professionals make diagnostic decisions based solely upon determining whether or not a particular child shows specified behaviors that indicate an ASD.

The American Psychiatric Association has written a book entitled the *Diagnostic and Statistical Manual of Mental Disorders*, Fourth Edition (DSM-IV). This manual spells out the specific behaviors that need to be present in order to consider diagnosing an autism spectrum disorder. Professionals should refer to the DSM-IV diagnostic criteria when assessing whether or not a particular child has an ASD. Chapters Four, Six, and Seven will provide more information about how a diagnostic evaluation may proceed and the specific behaviors that are assessed.

Each professional who evaluates a child may interpret these listed behaviors in his own way, which in turn can lead to differences of opinion regarding which (if any) autism spectrum disorder is present. For example, one of the diagnostic criterion for autistic disorder listed by the DSM-IV is "lack of social and emotional reciprocity." This phrase, not unlike many others in the DSM-IV, is relatively vague, even to the experts, and invites confusion. Another way personal interpretation can muddy the waters occurs when professionals over-focus on and exaggerate the importance of a particular behavior seen in many people with ASDs and make a diagnostic decision based on the presence or absence of this *one* behavior. For example, a pediatrician might say, "That child can't have autism—he makes eye contact," as if lack of eye contact is the sole prerequisite for a diagnosis. This type of attitude ignores the fact that diagnosing an autism spectrum disorder requires searching for *clusters* of behaviors which, when combined, indicate whether or not a diagnosis makes sense. A professional should recognize that a cluster, or grouping of behaviors, must be present, and one or two behaviors alone do not indicate an ASD. Chapter Four will detail the specific clusters of behaviors that must be present to warrant a diagnosis of each of the autism spectrum disorders.

Another reason for confusion in diagnosing autism spectrum disorders is the overlap among the diagnostic criteria of each disorder on the spectrum. For example, the diagnostic criteria for Asperger's disorder are almost identical to those listed for autistic disorder. Children with these disorders act very similarly and diagnostic confusion often occurs. To add to this confusion, Asperger's disorder has only been listed as an accepted diagnosis in the DSM since its fourth edition, published in 1994. So, there are older children with Asperger's disorder who were misdiagnosed prior to1994 because doctors weren't aware of this label. In addition, Asperger's disorder, being a relatively new diagnosis, seems to be the "diagnosis du jour." Many children with some social quirks and a few ritualistic behaviors are being wrongly diagnosed as having Asperger's disorder.

To muddle the situation further, many children show progress through the years, resulting in professionals revisiting their original diagnoses. Although a toddler may demonstrate behaviors that

> Diagnosing an autism spectrum disorder requires searching for *clusters* of behaviors which, when combined, indicate whether or not a diagnosis makes sense. A professional should recognize that a cluster, or grouping of behaviors, must be present, and one or two behaviors alone do not indicate an ASD.

are classically autistic, with intensive treatment, his behavior may improve to the point where another professional later determines that the same child, now older, has pervasive developmental disorder-not otherwise specified (PDD-NOS). Or, a professional may be hesitant to diagnose a very young child as having autistic disorder and therefore maintain he has PDD-NOS, only to determine when the child is older that a diagnosis of autistic disorder is actually warranted. It's no wonder people are so confused.

To avoid misdiagnosis, it's imperative that the professionals we entrust have experience in the field of ASDs and complete understanding of their diagnostic criteria. If a professional does not have comprehensive knowledge regarding ASDs, he may miss the diagnosis altogether or mislead parents by indicating that their child has a different diagnosis. Professionals with extensive experience in the area of ASDs can provide efficient and accurate assessment, which will quickly guide parents about their child's educational and treatment needs. In this age of busy household and work schedules, obtaining an efficient and accurate diagnosis is essential. This book aims to help you through the diagnostic maze and avoid its inherent pitfalls.

Remember the Kennedys from earlier in this chapter? They were unsure how to interpret the diagnoses given to their daughter, Kelly. Which diagnosis was "correct"? Did it matter? Professionals can also get caught up in the confusion if they are expected to make a diagnostic decision based upon less than adequate information and history, or if they don't have the experience to distinguish the various autism spectrum disorders. More importantly, children may be receiving inappropriate and inadequate treatment because misdiagnoses have taken place. This is especially worrisome because numerous research articles have shown that early diagnosis and treatment can make a significant difference in terms of eventual prognosis. For example, if a parent is consistently told not to worry that their child is "just a little slow" until the child reaches school age, the opportunities for early intervention have been lost. One goal of this book is to help you, as parents, avoid this fate. But remember, if your child is already school-age, it's not too late to get an appropriate diagnosis and begin on your journey through treatment toward a brighter future.

Summary

Our understanding of autism spectrum disorders is constantly evolving. Likewise, what we know about treatment and educational intervention for people on the autism spectrum is still developing. As parents, there will be times you will feel overwhelmed by all the jargon and various professionals involved in your child's care. You may become confused by the differing opinions regarding which diagnosis or treatment strategies make the most sense. As frustrating and potentially frightening as this process can be, it is my sincere hope that this book will arm you with what's necessary to critically evaluate what professionals tell you and shield you and your child from careless diagnoses. This book will provide you with *what you need to know* to make informed decisions on your child's behalf.

Each chapter in this book provides information about a particular area that is useful for you to explore. This introductory chapter provides some initial information about ASDs, why confusion exists, and why accurate diagnosis is so important. Chapter Two describes what symptoms to be on the lookout for and what to do if you are beginning to suspect that your child has an ASD. Chapter Three reviews the historical background of ASDs to allow a more comprehensive overview of where we have been and where the field stands currently. Chapter Four spells out the specific diagnostic criteria for each autism spectrum disorder, and Chapter Five denotes some common features of individuals with ASDs. Since there is much confusion surrounding the five types of ASDs, Chapter Six reviews the ways each ASD differs, using case studies to illustrate. Also addressed are conditions that share similar characteristics with ASDs and can create further confusion during the diagnostic process. Many parents will find Chapter Seven especially useful in that it describes what a diagnostic evaluation may entail and how to ensure your child is assessed fairly and accurately. Chapter Eight gives insight into the emotional reactions you might have to learning your child has an ASD and what practical steps can be taken. Finally, Chapter Nine reviews various treatments shown to be effective with many children with ASDs.

Parents Speak

No one cares for children as much as their parents.

We want our children to be all they can be and to have all the opportunities that life offers. I keep thinking of "Welcome to Holland," written by Emily Perl Kingsley. You've planned to go to Italy and somehow plans change—and you change—and after a time you realize that Holland is not such a bad place. You just learn to adjust.

Thirteen years into Jason's journey with health professionals and school systems, I have finally learned that I drive the bus, and they come along for the ride. I have learned to be Jason's voice, to remain firm in my convictions, to at least listen to people whose opinions I may not agree with, and to be patient. Jason's achievements are a direct result of his determination and hard work, the dedication of staff and professionals, the kindness of other children, the never ending compassion of his sister, and a relentless set of parents.

2 | So, You Suspect Your Child May Have An Autism Spectrum Disorder

The McLaughlin Family

Life with John and Elizabeth McLaughlin's only child, Anna, has been challenging since day one. After a difficult birth, Anna was placed in the neonatal intensive care unit for a few days of monitoring. As an infant, her behavior seemed ordinary except that she had difficulty tolerating certain milk formulas.

Of ongoing concern is the fact that she rarely sleeps through the night. Her interest in people seems to come and go. At times she responds to people's initiations to play, other times she seems oblivious to them. She loves to be tickled and swung by her father and will laugh uproariously when engaged in these activities. Her speech development seems fine in that she has a notable vocabulary; however, the rhythm of her speech seems odd. She enjoys playing with certain children and ignores others during play groups. At times she will throw a tantrum for what seems like hours while her parents stand by feeling helpless and overwhelmed.

During a recent family get-together, the McLaughlins were struck by the fact that Anna's behavior seemed so different than that of the other children her age. One relative even mentioned she thought Anna might have autism. Another relative chimed in saying Anna just needed some "good old-fashioned discipline."

As first-time parents, the McLaughlins are unsure as to whether their expectations for their child are unrealistic or whether there really is a serious problem with Anna's development. Now that she is almost two years old, Elizabeth and John are becoming increasingly concerned. Could she be deaf? Does she have mental retardation? Who should they talk to? Is their local pediatrician equipped to provide the answers they seek? What should they do next?

Are Your Concerns Like the McLaughlins'?

The McLaughlins' questions and emotional reactions are a very typical response to concerns your child might have autism. Your own family experience may be similar. As a parent, relative, friend, or professional who is questioning a child's development, it may be difficult to tell what is "normal" versus "abnormal" development. All children display unusual behaviors from time to time, especially when they are very young. They may bang their heads, be a bit of a "loner," insist on certain rituals, or flap their hands. Teasing out which of these behaviors indicate a developmental disorder, such as autism, versus behaviors that will fade over time can be a difficult task.

Most people are only familiar with Hollywood-style depictions of autism, with little knowledge about how this diagnosis could apply to their own child. You may assume that a child has to be nonverbal and rocking in a corner in order to be diagnosed with autism. Or, you may think all autistic children are exceptionally talented in math or the arts. From this perspective, it may seem senseless to compare the way your child thinks and behaves with such stereotypes.

If you are a parent or professional who is concerned that your child or a child you know may have an autism spectrum disorder, it is important to have a clear understanding of the developmental profile of children with ASDs as well as some basic knowledge of typical childhood development. A bit further along in this chapter is a list of typical developmental behaviors for two- and three-year-olds and behaviors that should raise suspicion. Knowing certain signs to look for as your child develops will help you avoid wasting precious time.

Recognizing Developmental Differences in Your Child

Some parents insist they knew something was different with their child from the moment they were born. Most parents of children who are eventually diagnosed with an ASD do not suspect any problems until their child is approaching their first or second birthday. However, parents may begin to notice that their child, by age one, is not consistently responsive to speech or has not even begun to babble. In some children, initial speech develops but then disappears. For example, by twelve or eighteen months, a child may be saying five to ten words but these words are lost by her second birthday. The child may not be pointing, or responding to her name being called. Eye contact may be fleeting. Some children may actively avoid snuggling and other types of physical contact. Unusual reactions to toys may be observed, such as lining them up in a repetitive manner, and spinning or flipping them in the air.

Various research studies have attempted to determine early signs of autism. One particularly interesting study involved comparing early videotapes of children who were eventually diagnosed with autism to videotapes of children who raised no developmental concerns (Osterling & Dawson, 1994; Baranek, 1999). The results of these studies indicate that certain factors tend to be quite effective in predicting which children are more likely to have an ASD and that these characteristics can be observed as early as their first birthday. The researchers identified behaviors that tend to be absent in the children eventually diagnosed with an ASD, including pointing, responding to one's name, eye contact, and bringing objects to others. Behaviors that are frequently more prevalent in these young children include excessive mouthing of objects, staring/fixating on objects, aversion to people touching them (e.g., hugging, snuggling), and a "flat" (i.e., unanimated) facial expression.

Although many parents begin to feel concerned when their child is an infant or toddler, the great majority of parents first seek professional assistance when they realize their child's speech development is delayed, around the age of two. This developmental difference seems to be the final push that prompts parents to recognize they can no longer ignore their child's atypical behaviors. Parents frequently have their child's hearing tested due to delayed speech and inconsistent responding to talking and noise. More often than not, hearing is found to be within the normal range and parents are left with more questions than answers.

Pursuing a diagnosis for your child is a courageous endeavor. While the answers to your questions may not be what you especially want to hear, gaining a fuller understanding of your child's development and individual needs will be worth the anxiety inherent in addressing the possibility of an ASD in the long run.

Developmental "Red Flags"

For those parents beginning to suspect their child may have an autism spectrum disorder, let's review certain behaviors and developmental trends that professionals see as "red flags." It is first important to point out that all children develop at varying rates. While one eighteen-month-old child may be speaking in two- to three-word sentences, another may still be using only one-word sentences to communicate her needs. However, both children would be exhibiting "typical" development. Although there is a wide range of "typical" development, it *is* possible to recognize when a child's development is falling significantly below the minimum expectation for her age group. Some unusual behaviors that may be acceptable for very young children can be a primary area of concern for older children. Please refer to the following table as a means of helping you determine if your child's development is outside the norm and suggestive of an autism spectrum disorder. ***This table is not meant to serve as a means to diagnose your child or replace the professionals, but rather for determining if you ought to pursue a full diagnostic workup for autism spectrum disorder.***

Table 2-1 | By Age Two...

You want to see...	"Red flags" that may suggest an autism spectrum disorder
Child enjoys being snuggled and held by familiar adults and responds to gentle physical contact as a means of calming. Child shows a wide range of facial expressions, including big smiles directed toward others during social interactions.	Child tends to avoid snuggling, squirms out of your grasp, or goes stiff. Tends to rely upon self-calming measures such as rocking or other repetitive behaviors rather than accepting nurturing from others. Facial expressions tend to be unanimated and smiles that do occur are usually not directly related to social interactions.
Child initiates and sustains eye contact.	Eye contact is brief and rarely initiated. Child may tend to look at others or objects via peripheral vision (i.e., out of the corner of her eye).
Child responds to own name when called.	Child inconsistently responds to own name being called. (Parents often worry that the child is deaf.)
Child is beginning to use basic gestures such as pointing, putting arms in the air to indicate a wish to be picked up, putting finger to lips while saying "Shhh," etc.	Child doesn't use basic gestures to communicate needs or wants. Instead, the child may whine or cry without any awareness that others need more information to discern her needs.
Child begins to speak in one-word sentences that are communicative in nature; i.e., the child is clearly attempting to communicate with others rather than just babbling.	Speech is absent or delayed. Sometimes child's speech may develop appropriately but is generally noncommunicative (e.g., she may repeat dialogues from videotapes to herself, known as "delayed echolalia").
Child is relatively flexible (when well-rested and content) regarding changes in routine or the environment.	Child finds even minor changes in routine or the environment discomforting. Responds with challenging behaviors such as prolonged tantrums or physical aggression.

(continued on next page)

Table 2-1 continued

You want to see...	"Red flags" that may suggest an autism spectrum disorder
Child begins to bring items to others or point out objects to share enjoyment or interest (e.g., points to a cow while making eye contact and says, "Cow!")	Child tends to bring items to others only when assistance is needed (e.g., brings cup when thirsty or broken toy that needs fixing). The child may take someone by the wrist and lead them to a desired object but then let go as soon as the person's purpose has been served. There is minimal enjoyment in sharing something that is exciting or interesting with others.
Child engages in appropriate concrete play activities (e.g., builds simple block structures, rocks baby doll, has figures "talk" to each other via babbling or short phrases). Child may not play interactively with others yet, aside from basic games like "chase." Child may tend to exhibit "parallel play," i.e., playing near peers without attempting to interact.	Child seems disinterested in most typical toys although finds objects (such as string, fans, etc.) engaging. May play with toys but in an unusual fashion (e.g., lines up blocks in a ritualistic manner, spins the wheels of toy trucks). May be especially adept at visual-motor tasks such as completing puzzles, stacking blocks into intricate towers, or matching objects.
Child is clearly aware of and interested in others in her environment. Initiates interactions. Responds differently to familiar versus unfamiliar people.	Child at times seems "in her own world" and oblivious to others. Does not become upset when left with an unfamiliar babysitter. Has not developed strong and personal relationships with family members.
Child is able to engage in various imitative activities and games such as "Peek-A-Boo" and "Wheels on the Bus."	Child shows minimal ability to imitate the actions of others.

Table 2-2 | By Age Three...

You want to see...	"Red flags" that may suggest an autism spectrum disorder
Child is beginning to develop strong relationships with certain peers and other familiar people such as preschool teachers or neighbors. May have a "best friend" as well as a few other close friends.	Child has not developed any strong attachments with peers. Tends to play alone. Will almost invariably actively avoid group activities.
Child is now speaking in full and relatively complicated sentences. Vocabulary is extensive and varied. She can communicate experiences. Speech continues to be clearly communicative in function. Uses common physical gestures to support communication (e.g., waving hello).	Child's speech continues to be delayed or is peculiar (e.g., child frequently insists on talking about the same topic repeatedly with little understanding of the give and take of a conversation). There may be some loss of previously used words. The quality of speech may be unusual, such as using a monotone or talking with an unusual rhythm.
Child engages in play activities that involve pretend play such as playing "house," being a super hero, etc. Play scenarios can be rather sophisticated and drawn out involving a clear plot. Child enjoys interactive play and will initiate games with peers.	Child's play style continues to be rather ritualistic and repetitive. Some pretend play may be existent but clearly reflects rote learning (i.e., the child is merely imitating a simple scenario that has been modeled by others or on TV or videos).
Child may exhibit some unusual behaviors but not frequently or repetitively. Although some young children may occasionally enjoy activities such as rocking, rubbing surfaces, or hand-flapping, they are able to be redirected to other activities easily.	Child spends prolonged periods of time engaged in repetitive movements that have no clear purpose. It may take a bit of effort to prompt child to stop, as she seems immersed in the behavior when it occurs.

If your child is four years of age or older, and you are observing many of the "red flags" listed above, it would be wise to pursue a comprehensive assessment.

Other "Red Flags" to be On the Lookout For:

- Startling easily;
- Echolalia, that is, repeating words or phrases that she's heard. This could involve repeating words immediately (e.g., when you ask her, "Do you want a cookie?," she responds, "Want a cookie?"), or at a later time (repeating dialogue from videotapes that she's watched previously);
- Expressive speech may involve repeating the same words or phrases over and over again to herself or to others (known as "perseverative speech");
- The child may have difficulty understanding and following simple instructions. Or, she may seem to understand a given instruction today but appear oblivious to its meaning tomorrow;
- Sleep issues, such as disrupted sleep, including an inability to fall asleep in her bed, awakening during the night and staying awake for prolonged periods of time, and seeming to need much less sleep than would be expected;
- High levels of distractibility;
- Limited awareness of dangerous situations (e.g., may climb out onto the roof, repeatedly attempt to touch light sockets or the stovetop, run into the street without any thought to oncoming cars);
- Mood swings that appear to be "out of the blue" and difficult to understand;
- Physical aggression against others that can at times seem random and inexplicable;
- Self-injurious behaviors, such as hitting her head, biting her hands, or slapping her face;

- Over- or under-reactions to sensory input, such as a high tolerance for pain, smelling or licking objects, upset over mechanical noises, refusal to wear clothes that are a certain texture or style, putting her hands over her ears in reaction to particular noises, etc.;
- Limited food preferences (e.g., will only eat/drink a few specific items);
- Inability to "warm up" to others no matter how much time has passed;
- For children aged five or older, there is a difficulty taking others' perspective and understanding that other people don't think or feel exactly as they do. (Keep in mind that even children under five years who are typically developing have difficulty with this concept.)

Again, the above charts are merely meant to provide a broad framework for helping parents determine whether or not a diagnostic work-up is warranted for their child. Only a comprehensive assessment, as described in Chapter Seven, will lead to a definitive diagnostic decision.

Perhaps your child has already been diagnosed with another disorder such as mental retardation, Down Syndrome, cerebral palsy, a hearing impairment, or a speech/language delay. When a child has a preexisting condition and begins to demonstrate features that may indicate an ASD, parents and professionals often have difficulty teasing out which symptoms are specific to the already existent disorder and which may be linked to an ASD. The presence of an already-existing disorder does not rule out the possibility of an ASD, but it can make its diagnosis more difficult. As will be explained more fully in Chapter Six, it is not uncommon for a child to have more than one diagnosis (termed "comorbidity").

> The presence of an already-existing disorder, such as Down syndrome or a speech/language delay, does not rule out the possibility of an ASD, but it can make its diagnosis more difficult.

In the case of Anna McLaughlin at the beginning of this chapter, we can see there are various "red flags" that warrant her parents pursuing a comprehensive evaluation. For example, her interest in others "comes and goes." Although this may very well be merely a reflection of Anna's personality, completely ignoring others' initiations is a relatively uncommon behavior in young children. Her odd speech patterns are also a "red flag," but by no means proof positive that she has an autism spectrum disorder. Young children often generate idiosyncratic language, such as making up their own words to describe an object or action. Sleep disturbances and mood swings are not uncommon in children with ASDs and Anna certainly displays these two tendencies. However, toddlers in general can be moody and poor sleepers. Although the overall description of Anna is insufficient to make a definitive diagnosis, there are enough "red flags" to warrant further investigation.

If you suspect your child may have an ASD, it may prove useful to review the list of "red flags" with another person who knows your child well, such as your spouse, your child's teacher, or a pediatrician. Although there is no "magic number" of symptoms that need to be present in order to warrant a more comprehensive diagnostic evaluation, if you feel that many of the descriptions listed above sound like your child, it is important for you to pursue the issue. When reading through the above descriptions of "red flags" and behavioral characteristics indicative of an ASD, you may begin to berate yourself for not having picked up on some subtle cues that your child demonstrated early on. Keep in mind that all children demonstrate a wide range of developmental trends and therefore it is difficult for any parent to know what is "typical" or "atypical." Rather than dwelling on possible missed signs, focus on your child's present needs and recognize that an accurate diagnosis at any age will facilitate your child's progress and help you find appropriate interventions.

Taking Action

At some point, many parents experience a gradual dawning that their child's development may in fact be significantly impaired. At times, a relative or professional, such as a preschool teacher, may introduce the possibility of autism. Parents often bring their concerns to their child's pediatrician, with varying results. Although some pediatricians have the experience and knowledge to definitively rule in or rule out an ASD, the majority do not. Unfortunately, it is not uncommon for pediatricians to discount parents' concerns, especially if this is their first child or she is under the age of two. If you feel that your pediatrician is being unresponsive to your questions, I highly recommend you seek a second opinion. As described in detail in Chapter Seven, in order to sort through the confusion, it is usually best to seek a diagnostic evaluation conducted by a multidisciplinary team specializing in autism spectrum disorders.

If you decide to get a second opinion, gather the names of possible diagnostic teams from local support groups or agencies that focus on autism spectrum disorders. Ask parents of children with ASDs what their experiences were in these varying settings. It may prove worthwhile to ask professionals at your local school system or ARC for the names of support groups or agencies in your community. An Internet search may also help you obtain the addresses of well-respected diagnostic settings that are within driving distance of your home. Various resources can be found at the end of this book that will help you locate a place you can take your child to receive a thorough and competent assessment.

As described in Chapter Seven, there are a variety of places you can find diagnostic teams, including hospitals, clinics, schools, and universities. You may or may not feel comfortable informing your child's pediatrician that you are seeking a second opinion. This is a personal decision that is yours to make. One advantage of keeping your pediatrician informed is that she can be an integral part of the treatment plan once a definitive diagnosis is made.

Also, your pediatrician can share your child's medical file with the new evaluator, thus providing more information to tap for developing a diagnosis. Although you may have a positive relationship with your pediatrician and hesitate to seek a second opinion, you need to remember that you are a consumer and your child's strongest advocate, and therefore should do what you feel is in your child's best interest. Continuing to explore what is underlying your child's atypical development is a courageous endeavor and should not be hindered by concerns of hurting your pediatrician's feelings.

What Will a Diagnosis Mean for Our Child?

If you are considering the possibility that your child may have an ASD, you probably have many general questions regarding this condition. For example, you may be wondering what such a diagnosis would *mean* for your child's overall development and prognosis. In general, having an autism spectrum disorder implies that:

■ Your child will likely require specialized educational services (at least initially) in order to progress successfully. It may be necessary to use intensive 1:1 teaching strategies with your child, rather than assuming most learning will occur passively, as seen in typically developing youngsters.

■ Your child may have difficulty processing information and understanding what is said to her.

■ Your child may exhibit unusual behaviors that do not make sense to you and others.

■ Your child's social interactions may be limited or unusual.

■ Your child's speech will likely be delayed. The great majority of children with ASDs eventually learn to communicate either through speech, signing, or using an augmentative method, such as exchanging pictures that depict their message.

- Your child may rely on challenging behaviors to express frustration over not being able to communicate her needs.
- Although all children with ASDs show some degree of progress as they grow, the core elements of the diagnosis (e.g., qualitative impairments in social and language skills) tend to remain apparent throughout their lives. For example, while a high functioning adult with autistic disorder may be able to maintain employment and live independently, she may not particularly enjoy social situations and remain somewhat of a "loner."

In terms of prognosis, there is no way to know for certain what lies ahead for any given child. Be very skeptical if a professional tells you that your young child will "never" accomplish certain developmental goals. Many parents whose children have been diagnosed with ASDs have enjoyed proving these naysayers wrong when their child accomplishes the "impossible." Even if your child has a secondary diagnosis, such as mental retardation or cerebral palsy, it is premature for any professional to dictate your child's future, especially when the child is young. Given the relative successes that we've seen with current treatment strategies, you have every reason to not only retain hope regarding your child's future, but work toward making it even brighter.

What About Our Other Kids?

Parents who already have one child with an autism spectrum disorder often worry about the development of subsequent children. This concern is understandable and valid given that ASDs appear to have a genetic underpinning. That is, if one child in the family has an ASD, there is a slightly higher possibility that siblings will also have developmental differences or even an autism spectrum disorder. For more information on the theories of the cause(s) of autism, refer to Chapter Three. If one of your children has already been diagnosed with an autism spectrum disorder, you will want to be extra aware of your other children's development, keeping an eye out for the early signs of ASD. Does your other child respond to her name? Is her language development appropriate? How are her social skills? In sum, refer to the charts above as a guide to assessing the likelihood that your younger child also has an autism spectrum disorder.

It is important to emphasize that if you have one child with an autism spectrum disorder, the likelihood you will have another child with ASD is very slight. Approximately two to three percent of siblings of children with ASDs also have one. If developmental differences *do* occur, they are usually relatively mild, such as a speech delay or social awkwardness. However, the great majority of siblings show typical development with no signs of an ASD whatsoever. Therefore, there is no need to rush your other children to a developmental specialist unless you have actual concerns that prompt you to question the possibility of an ASD or other developmental difference.

Having additional children once one of your children has been diagnosed with an ASD is a very personal decision. Some parents find the possibility of having another child with ASD to be so overwhelming that they actively avoid any future pregnancies. This concern is especially warranted if a specific genetic abnormality has been identified in your child with an ASD (e.g., fragile X syndrome). Other parents are willing to assume the somewhat elevated risk of having a second child with a developmental difference. It is essential to discuss the issue thoroughly and honestly with your spouse and professionals in the field before making a final decision.

Parents Speak

We first noticed that something was wrong with our son when we saw repetitive behavior (i.e., opening and closing sliding glass doors a lot, turning light switches on and off all the time), stubborn behavior, misuse of pronouns, and parallel play. We questioned our son's pediatrician and his response was, "He's a strong willed child." When these behaviors continued, I grew very upset and in tears one night I said to my husband, "Something is wrong." He agreed and we went back to the pediatrician. This time he took our concerns more seriously.

⟲

When my sons were little I didn't worry, but when I helped a friend research autism to answer questions about her children, I couldn't help but notice that our twin boys exhibited some autistic symptoms (lining up objects, spinning toys). The most significant sign was that they started saying "Mama" about age one and a half and then suddenly stopped. This raised a red flag as I was their primary stay-at-home caregiver, and "Mom" just wasn't a part of their vocabulary. At that point I contacted our pediatrician, who sent us to see a specialist.

⟲

When Juliet was two and a half, we started to see things that concerned us. When I would pick her up from daycare, she would just be sitting there waiting for me, and would not be playing like the other kids. This was a change, as she used to have pretty good play skills.

⟲

Birthday number two, three, and four went by and each time people would say, "His dad was quiet too. He'll talk soon." As he'd blow out the candles, I'd always pray, "Just let this be the year he speaks." Andrew just turned sixteen. My annual wish still hasn't changed.

3 | Autism: History, Myths, Progress, Demographics, and Theories of Cause

The Ryan Family

Life in the 1950s: Marie and Frank Ryan perceived themselves as a typical American family. Frank went to work each day while Marie stayed home with their two children, Frances (age eight) and Billy (age three). All seemed fine until they began to notice Billy had some unusual play behaviors. He liked to line toys up in a repetitive manner and became very upset if anyone moved a toy even slightly. He tended to rock his body back and forth for long periods of time while moaning. He seemed only mildly interested in other people and instead was drawn to spinning objects, such as the desk fan in their den. By age three, he could only say a few words.

When Marie and Frank took Billy to their pediatrician to determine what was wrong, the doctor was equally puzzled and took a "wait and see" attitude. Over the next two years, the Ryans sought the advice of a neurologist and child psychologist, but neither were able to provide any answers. The Ryans tried diligently to "break through Billy's shell" to no avail. When he turned five, Billy went to kindergarten. Unfortunately, the teachers were unable to manage his behavior, labeled him "unteachable," and asked that his parents not return him to school. The Ryans were devastated and again left to their own devices. They attempted to teach him the best they could at home with little support from the educational system.

When Billy was seven years old, the Ryans heard about a child psychiatrist in a neighboring state who specialized in children with unusual development. They had to drive three hours to reach the psychiatrist's office, but were eager about the possibility of finally understanding Billy's troubles. After a prolonged assessment including various tests and a review of Billy's developmental history, the specialist determined that Billy had "infantile autism." The specialist told the Ryans, in a rather matter-of-fact manner, that they were to blame for Billy's condition and that the only viable treatment was to place Billy in a residential institution away from his family.

Marie and Frank were both outraged and afraid! What was "infantile autism"? What could they have possibly done to cause their son's developmental differences? They knew that they were loving, honest parents and that they had treated Billy no differently than Frances. Although none of this seemed to make any sense, after many heartbreaking discussions, the Ryans decided the experts knew best and placed Billy in a local institution. Every time they drove past the facility, Marie would break down in tears, feeling overwhelmed by guilt and longing for her little boy.

This scenario sounds like a scene from a horror movie, but, unfortunately, it reflects the norm for assessing and treating children with autism in the mid-twentieth century. Fortunately, we have come a long way in understanding autism since then. Let's review the historical background of autism spectrum disorders to gain a greater appreciation of the strides we have made over the past sixty years. It's useful to understand how the diagnosis of autism was initially defined and treated as well as the cultural factors that have influenced our perceptions of people with autism over the years.

History of Autism

Leo Kanner First Coins the Term "Autism"

Autism was first described in the early 1940s by Leo Kanner, a child psychiatrist at Johns Hopkins University Medical School in Baltimore, Maryland. Kanner described the group of eleven children he treated, all of whom demonstrated similar behavioral characteristics. These included extreme social isolation or withdrawal, communication difficulties, and ritualistic behaviors. The development of this new diagnostic category was groundbreaking. In fact, many of the behaviors described by Kanner are incorporated into present-day diagnostic criteria, influencing our thinking about autism still today.

Kanner coined the label "autistic," borrowing the term from early descriptions of people with schizophrenia, who were socially withdrawn or "in their own world." As a consequence, for many years, schizophrenia and autism were mistakenly thought to be related conditions. In the early days, children diagnosed with autism were often re-diagnosed with schizophrenia once they reached adulthood. Needless to say, this was quite confusing for everyone involved, especially parents.

Early Theories About Autism

Initially, although Kanner was correct in hypothesizing that autism was due to abnormalities in the brain, other professionals of the time, such as Bruno Bettleheim, hypothesized that autism was the result of poor parenting. He proposed that due to ineffective parenting, certain unfortunate children found their world hostile and scary, causing them to have unusual behaviors (Yeung-Courchesne & Courchesne, 1997). As with the Ryan family, parents (especially mothers) were most often blamed for their child's disorder. Professionals even used the phrase "refrigerator mothers" to describe these women whom they believed were cold and unfeeling toward their children. Intervention therefore required a "parentectomy," that is, remove the children from the parents and the autism will presumably be cured. Interactions with parents were limited by removing the children from the home and placing them in institutions. In an effort to convince the children with ASDs that the world was indeed safe, an accepting, nurturing environment was provided within a residential setting. Not surprisingly, this treatment strategy only led to heightened parental guilt, confusion for the child, and no decrease in autistic behaviors.

Needless to say, this attitude caused quite a lot of unnecessary pain to the parents of children with autism in the 1940s through the 1960s. Not only did they have to worry about their child's unusual development, but they were told *they* were to blame. To his credit, Kanner recognized that there were most likely physiological, as opposed to psychological, reasons for the children's unusual development. Eventually, research showed that parents of children with autism were equally competent and loving parents compared to the general population. But, why then were some parents of children with autism less physically demonstrative? Professionals realized there was a "chicken and egg" problem at hand: Was it because the parents were inherently cold and unfeeling, or because their child cried or screamed every time they attempted to show them physical affection? Many children with ASDs find physical touch unpleasant, and therefore their parents' behavior is "shaped" to refrain from snuggling and giving hugs. Professionals ultimately realized that the parents of kids with autism were, in fact, quite affectionate with their other children, thus disproving the idea that they were cold and unloving.

In the early 1960s, Bernard Rimland was one of the initial pioneers to promote the idea that autism was due to abnormalities in the brain rather than poor parenting (Rimland, 1964). As a professional in the field as well as the father of a son with autism, Rimland had a vested interest in investigating the underlying reasons for this disorder. His hypothesis that autism is actually a neurologically based syndrome was gradually adopted and has inspired numerous scientific studies over the years.

A pioneer in the treatment of individuals with ASDs who also emerged in the 1960s was O. Ivar Lovaas at the University of California-Los Angeles (UCLA). Lovaas developed behavioral treatments that demonstrated children with ASDs could learn given a highly structured environment where rewards and punishments were provided in a consistent manner (Lovaas & Simmons, 1969). Speech improved and aggressive tendencies in children with ASDs diminished when these new behavioral principles were applied to teaching techniques. These studies constituted a notable breakthrough, resulting in renewed hope for parents and professionals regarding the overall prognosis for children with autism. As will be reviewed in Chapter Nine, many of Lovaas' theories and "behavioral treatments" continue to influence contemporary interventions.

Fortunately, by the 1970s, separating children with ASDs from their parents was no longer the treatment of choice. During this period, specialized schools were developed, with staff trained in the use of "behavioral techniques," which are discussed in more detail in Chapter Nine. At times, the punishment techniques utilized were overly harsh, including slapping a child's thigh or hand. Fortunately, much emphasis was placed on providing the children with frequent positive rewards for the demonstration of desired behaviors and the data reflected slow but notable progress. Also, school personnel recognized that parents were essential members of the treatment team rather than the "cause" of their child's developmental differences. Parents were taught to implement behavioral strategies in the home in order to provide a more consistent experience for their children. Many of the pioneers of the 1960s and 1970s are the forefathers of the effective and state-of-the-art treatment methods practiced today.

Myths

There are several myths about ASDs that have been maintained over the years even though they have no support from scientific research. The following are examples.

Myth: "Parents cause autism."

As we discussed above, this myth has been disproved again and again. However, there are still many people who mistakenly believe that children with autism must have experienced some traumatic event in their lives (usually assumed to be due to poor parenting or abuse). It is important for parents of children with

ASDs to remind themselves that they did *not* cause their child's disorder. Most parents of children with autism are loving and supportive. Of course, there are also parents of children with ASDs who can be abusive or less than loving; however, the incidence of this is no greater than in the general population of parents.

Myth: "Children with autism are, in fact, 'idiot savants.'"

That is, children with ASDs are believed to have incredible cognitive abilities or seemingly unattainable skills. Movies such as "Rainman," while entertaining and realistic in some ways, perpetuate the myth that individuals with autism are hidden geniuses. More recent media productions have also implied that people with ASDs have uncanny skills and therefore many people continue to believe this myth. Although some individuals with ASDs (especially those with Asperger's disorder) show a remarkable ability to memorize facts regarding a particular topic, the truth remains that most people with autism do not have any unusual splinter skills.

One reason this myth may have been perpetuated is that individuals with ASDs demonstrate wide ranges of skills across various developmental areas. For example, they may be completely nonverbal but able to complete a complicated puzzle. If you remember from the introduction, the term "pervasive developmental disorder" is currently being replaced by the more apt phrase "autism spectrum disorder"; however, the earlier designation still fits the diagnosis in many ways. Inconsistencies across skill areas are expected because people with ASDs have a pervasive developmental *disorder* rather than a pervasive developmental *delay*. The fact that their development is "disordered" means their skills do not develop in the sequence you would expect. For example, a six-year-old child may be able to list every character of a "Star Wars" movie but be unable to label simple objects. The knowledge regarding "Star Wars" may seem like a relative sign of genius when compared to the child's inability to label objects, contributing to the myth of the "idiot savant."

Myth: "Children with ASDs are more prevalent in families with higher socio-economic status."

In fact, one of the more recent versions of the American Psychiatric Association's Diagnostic Statistical Manual (DSM-III-R), published in 1987, implied that this myth was true. However, the facts just do not support this contention. This misnomer was most likely generated early on when only a handful of professionals were sufficiently experienced in diagnosing children with autism. It is highly probable that the only parents who could afford to travel to these specialized clinics and pay these doctors' high prices were relatively wealthy. We now know that autism spectrum disorders occur across all races, socio-economic groups, and cultures.

Progress Through the Years

As the years have passed, various truisms have emerged:

- Although the jury is still out as to what exactly causes them, recent studies clearly indicate autism spectrum disorders are organically based conditions. In other words, they are a result of nature and not nurture, as once thought. It is becoming more and more clear through the years that ASDs are due to abnormalities in the brain rather than to any environmental factors such as poor parenting.
- The diagnostic criteria for each of the autism spectrum disorders have been fine-tuned and characteristics for each subcategory have gotten more specific in recent years. This will be discussed in more detail in Chapters Four and Six.
- Professionals are more adept at recognizing ASDs in young children, which is especially important considering that overall prognosis is improved when a child receives early intervention by age four or five (see Chapter Nine).

- Parents are no longer blamed for their child's condition but rather are seen as an essential part of the treatment team.
- The general public has become more educated about the existence of ASDs through heightened media awareness and knowledge.
- People now recognize that the symptoms of ASDs do not just "disappear" when children reach the age of twenty-one. Children with autism become adults with autism.
- The specific terms used to describe these children (i.e., Kanner's syndrome, infantile autism, pervasive developmental disorder) have changed through the years in an attempt to better describe and understand the characteristics and needs of people with ASDs.

Demographic Data About ASDs

Incidence

The incidence of reported cases of autism spectrum disorders has risen dramatically over the past few decades. In the 1960s, the incidence was cited as 5 to 15 in 10,000 births. More recent studies have indicated a sharp rise in the incidence of ASDs. For example, recent studies in California suggest as many as 1 in 500 individuals have an autism spectrum disorder (Croen, Grether, Hoogstrate, & Selvin, 2002). Some parents and professionals believe that environmental factors, such as immunizations, may have caused the notable increase in numbers. However, thus far there are no clear data to support any consistent environmental factors that may have contributed to the increase in cases of ASD.

Other people believe that the increase in reported cases of autism spectrum disorders is inflated due to various factors. For example, more pediatricians, psychologists, and other evaluators are now trained in recognizing ASDs and are therefore more likely to diagnose and report it. Also, the diagnostic criteria in each new revision of the Diagnostic Statistical Manual (DSM) have provided ever-widening diagnostic criteria, which increases the number of children who fall within the spectrum. For instance, the newest revision of the DSM includes five types of ASDs as compared to only two in the previous version. Although the heightened awareness, expertise, and broadened diagnostic umbrella can account for some of the increased frequency in ASDs, there is still no doubt that the overall incidence of ASDs is of epidemic proportions for reasons unknown.

Gender Ratios

As is the case with many developmental differences, there is a higher incidence of ASDs in males compared to females. It is generally thought that autism is four times more likely to occur in males than females. However, the male:female difference is less pronounced in children who are less adept. For children with ASDs whose IQs are in the severe or profound range of mental retardation, the gender ratio is closer to two times as many males as females.

Age of Onset

With the exception of childhood disintegrative disorder, the behaviors inherent to an ASD must be present prior to three years of age to warrant the diagnosis. (Please refer to Chapter Four for a comprehensive review of each ASD as well as the diagnostic criteria for each.) The diagnosis can be made when the child is older, but it is essential that information regarding the child's early development is included in the diagnostic evaluation to assure there were signs early on.

Overlap with Mental Retardation

The majority of people with autism spectrum disorders test in the mentally retarded range on traditional intelligence tests. A diagnosis of mental retardation is warranted if an individual receives a score of seventy or below on an IQ test, plus demonstrates significant difficulties with daily living skills, such as dressing, bathing, or participating in the community. According to standard IQ tests, a minority of individuals with ASDs have average or above average intellectual ability. While it is likely that many children with ASDs do in fact have mental retardation in addition to an autism spectrum disorder, we should keep in mind that traditional IQ tests are often not the best assessment method.

Tapping a child's cognitive skills is difficult under any circumstances, but particularly if the child has an ASD and is under five years of age. These tests tend to be *socially biased* and *language-biased*. That is, a child needs to have relatively advanced social and language skills to understand what is being asked of him and respond appropriately. As we will review in Chapter Four, social and language skills are two areas of particular difficulty for people with ASDs. Due to these inherent biases, it is likely that young children with ASDs are unable to perform to the best of their ability during testing, resulting in IQ scores that are an underestimation of their actual intellectual abilities. Consequently, many of these children are deemed "untestable" by evaluators, and intelligence is estimated via behavioral observations and teacher report. In children with ASDs, who are over the age of six, IQ test results are typically more representative of their true cognitive skills and impairments. If the test is given repeatedly across years, those results should be consistent over time. For a more in-depth discussion of ASDs and IQ tests, see Chapter Seven.

Theories of Cause

As mentioned earlier, early theories pointed to parents as the underlying cause of autism. Fortunately, this theory has since been disproved and parents no longer have to feel the weight of guilt brought on by misinformed professionals. But, what *does* cause autism spectrum disorders? Unfortunately, no one yet knows exactly what causes autism spectrum disorders. There are most likely many reasons why a child develops an ASD. This is the case with many developmental disabilities, such as mental retardation. To illustrate, a child with mental retardation may have ingested lead paint that caused brain damage; another child may have mental retardation due to brain damage resulting from a terrible car accident. In the area of autism spectrum disorders, various factors have been suggested as possible underlying causes. The following is a brief description of the most commonly cited theories:

Genetic Predisposition

Studies indicate that there is a familial pattern, or genetic input, in the development of autism spectrum disorders. Plainly stated, autism tends to run in families, therefore suggesting that there may be a genetic cause. Studies of twins show that identical twins are more likely to both have ASDs, although fraternal twins are no more likely to share the condition. Studies such as these provide support for the belief that there is a genetic underpinning to autism.

Although most siblings of children with ASDs develop typically, there is a two to three percent chance that they too will have an ASD. Sometimes siblings do not demonstrate the full battery of behavioral differences but instead show subtle developmental differences, such as language delays or social awkwardness.

Central Nervous System Involvement

Most professionals in the field believe that children with ASDs have abnormalities in the central nervous system; that is, within the nervous system located in the brain (Gillberg & Coleman, 2000). The brain has approximately one hundred billion special cells called neurons that enable its various parts to communicate with one another, to receive input from the rest of the body, and to send information to the rest of the body. When there are flaws in these connections, many symptoms can occur, including difficulty controlling parts of the body, and problems with processing and understanding information. The central nervous system differences seen in children with ASDs may directly affect their ability to communicate or interact socially. These differences may also contribute to the rituals and repetitive behaviors seen in many people with ASDs.

Some research studies have focused on the way information is transferred between nerves in the brains of people in the general population. Information in our brains is transmitted to other cells in our body via rapid sequences of nerves being "fired," or activated. When a nerve cell is activated, it releases a chemical (called a neurotransmitter) that in turn activates other nerves, until the message reaches its final destination. Scientists have hypothesized that there may be either excessive or depleted levels of neurotransmitters in some children with autism spectrum disorders. For instance, these children may have unusually high levels of a neurotransmitter called serotonin, which can be controlled with medications called Selective Serotonin Reuptake Inhibitors (SSRIs). By modulating the amount of serotonin in the brain, scientists think the central nervous system can operate more efficiently and effectively. This, along with other types of treatment methods, will be discussed in greater detail in Chapter Nine.

Other studies have focused on magnetic resonance images (MRIs) as a way to look at how the brains of children with ASDs compare to the brains of typically developing children. An MRI involves taking a "picture" of the central nervous system structure and looking for unusual patterns of activity in brain chemistry. During an MRI, the individual typically lies down on a table that slides into a large container. An MRI usually takes thirty to sixty minutes and therefore can be discomforting for some people. Often, earphones are provided so that the individual can listen to music to help them tolerate the procedure. Open MRI machines are less confining and may be an option if your child finds a more traditional MRI to be too anxiety-provoking.

MRI research studies have indicated that there are often structural differences in the brains of people with autism (Courchesne, et al., 1988; Sparks, et al., 2002). The researchers have focused on certain areas of the brain that show abnormalities. More recently, Eric Courchesne and his colleagues reported that children with autistic disorder tend to have a smaller head circumference than average at birth (in the twenty-fifth percentile), but then show rapid head growth within the first year or so of life, such that their head circumference is on average in the eighty-fifth percentile by the time they are eighteen months old (Courchesne, 2003). They contend that such rapid brain growth makes learning difficult in the first year of life because the fast pace may create abnormal neural connections that make it very difficult for children with autistic disorder to take in information efficiently and successfully. Although this type of research has not yet led to any treatment strategies, the results support the contention that ASDs are associated with abnormalities in brain structure and development.

Similarly, some studies have shown that a small percentage of children with ASDs have atypical electroencephalogram, or EEG, results. However, there is no clear pattern among these children's results and most children with ASDs do not have unusual EEG readings. Interestingly, autopsies have shown that the brains of some individuals with autism spectrum disorders are heavier than usual (Bauman & Kemper, 1994), implying that there may be *too many* nerves in the central nervous system, producing a virtual "traffic jam" of messages in the brain. This could explain why children with ASDs have difficulty interpreting the information they receive from the environment, which in turn makes it difficult for them to behave and communicate effectively.

Immunization Shots

One of the more recent and controversial hypotheses developed regarding the root of ASDs is that they are caused by immunization shots typically given to toddlers (Wakefield, 1998). The vaccinations that have drawn the most attention are the ones that contained a mercury-based preservative called Thimerosal (e.g., the vaccine against measles, mumps, and rubella, or MMR). Some people were concerned that the vaccines with Thimerosal may in fact be producing mercury poisoning in young children, even though these vaccines only contained a very small amount of mercury. As a precautionary measure, in 1999 the U.S. Public Health Service, the American Academy of Pediatrics, and vaccine manufacturers agreed that Thimerosal should no longer be used in vaccines for children.

Although one or two studies seem to imply that the introduction of the measles virus via the shot may adversely affect children's intestines, the majority of research indicates that there is no cause-effect relationship between immunizations and the incidence of ASDs (Dales, et al., 2001). The American Medical Association's position supports the claim that immunizations do *not* cause autism. Parents may inadvertently link MMR immunizations with the onset of autism because these shots are usually administered at about the same time their child first develops obvious signs of autism (e.g., delays in language development). Rather than being a *cause* of autism, the link with MMR immunizations may be a timing coincidence that has misled parents and professionals.

Possible Contributing Medical Conditions

Although no clear pattern of medical conditions has emerged among people with ASDs, there is a higher likelihood that they will have a history of encephalitis, phenylketonuria, tuberous sclerosis, maternal use of cocaine during pregnancy, or anoxia (loss of oxygen) during birth, compared to those not affected by autism. It may be that the presence of one or more of these factors may lead to the development of an ASD in fetuses that are already predisposed to autism in some manner.

Concluding Remarks About Possible Causes of Autism

Although many theories exist about the cause(s) of autism spectrum disorders, no one theory addresses all of autism's unanswered questions. This can be very frustrating for parents because understanding the cause(s) of autism may provide guidance regarding treatment as well as whether or not they want to have additional children. Parents understandably feel pressured to adopt a theory and try relatively new treatment strategies that have not yet been proven to work. As one mother once said, "I don't have five years to wait until the research supports or disclaims each treatment method. I need to help my child *now*!" While it is understandably tempting to latch on to the promise of a new theory, it is important that parents remain cautious and objective in their quest to uncover the causes of their child's condition. If you spend undue time chasing a questionable "cure," you may inadvertently lessen the time spent exploring a more effective, time-proven intervention for your child.

As you read this book, various researchers around the world are conducting additional studies in order to gain a better understanding of the underlying cause(s) of autism spectrum disorders (e.g., genetic studies, brain research). It is advantageous for parents to keep abreast of this research in order to ascertain if the results could apply to their child. Many parents also find it useful to participate in local studies so that they can be up to date regarding the findings. Only through such dedicated, data-driven scientific study will we be able to gain a better understanding of the "whys" of autism spectrum disorders.

Parents Speak

There is this feeling that you're being punished for something you did years ago, like maybe you caused the autism. You never stop thinking about it and wondering "Why me?," "Why my kid?" I feel afraid for us and afraid for her.

༺ঔৎ༻

When I told our pediatrician my concerns about Patrick, especially his language development, she very nonchalantly said that he had "autistic qualities." The very cold doctor then said that Patrick "wasn't like the 'Rainman,'" but he needed further evaluation. She offered no more information or reassurance but promptly referred me to a specialist who had a three-month waiting list.

4 | Breaking Down the Five Autism Spectrum Disorders

The Vance Family

Tessa and Bob Vance were excited when they found out they were having another child. Although their first child, Ellie, was only eighteen months old, they figured the two children would play well together due to their close proximity in age. Little Kate was born after a rather prolonged labor. The doctors said she was deprived of oxygen briefly during delivery but that there should be no serious problems as a result. Much to her parents' relief, Kate's early developmental milestones, such as sitting up and walking, occurred right on time.

By the time Kate was one and a half years old, however, her parents' fears returned. She was unresponsive to their attempts to engage her and, what's more, she rarely smiled. Kate had recurring ear infections and her parents felt they were virtually living at the pediatrician's office. Although Kate had said a few words at an early age, such as "mama" and "up," by the age of two, all speech had disappeared. Her parents worried that the ear infections had produced permanent hearing loss, but testing ruled this out.

In contrast to their images of Kate and Ellie playing joyfully together, Kate had little interest in playing with toys or her sister. In fact, Kate would periodically become quite aggressive towards Ellie, and her parents consequently felt the need to supervise them at all times. If left to her own devices, Kate would spend hours staring at herself in reflective surfaces while twirling in circles. She also showed certain "obsessions," for example, she insisted on going through the McDonald's drive-through and would become intensely upset if her *parents refused to do so. Unfortunately, they couldn't avoid passing the McDonald's on their way home. What seemed especially unusual to her parents was the fact that Kate did not seem particularly interested in buying or eating the fast food; rather, the mere act of going through the drive-through was what interested her. If the McDonald's was closed, Kate was quite content to have her parents go through the drive-through and pretend to order.*

Kate's parents shared their concerns with their pediatrician, who admitted he had little experience with children like Kate. He pointed out that Ellie may be "talking for" Kate and that this may have stunted her language growth. The Vances were dissatisfied with this explanation and requested a second opinion. The pediatrician referred them to a nearby diagnostic team that specialized in atypical childhood development. As part of the evaluation, the diagnostic team reviewed a wide variety of Kate's behaviors with the Vances. They used unfamiliar terms such as "self-stimulatory behaviors" and "noncommunicative speech." The evaluators asked if Kate had lost any skills. They measured her head and evaluated her motor coordination in an attempt to determine which, if any, ASD diagnosis was warranted. After reviewing the diagnostic criteria for each of the autism spectrum disorders, the diagnostic team decided that Kate displayed behavioral symptoms of autistic disorder.

Fortunately, Tessa and Bob had anticipated this diagnosis and had already researched setting up an intensive teaching program in their home. Through a local parent support group, they had learned that such a home-program could be implemented under the supervision of a university-based team from out of state, and they developed a comprehensive treatment plan whereby Kate would obtain 40 hours per week of 1:1 Applied Behavior Analysis (ABA) training. They recruited instructors from a local college and the university team provided periodic training workshops. With some help from a social worker they connected with through their contacts at the local ARC, the Vances became eligible for funding that helped offset the cost of such a venture. Kate also received speech and occupational therapies through the local early intervention system. Within one year, Kate was speaking in full sentences and showing signifi-

cantly improved social skills. Although she still showed some developmental delays, her parents were optimistic about her future.

During the comprehensive diagnostic evaluation, the Vances were exposed to many terms and were asked many questions about Kate's development. In essence, they received a "mini-lesson" on the characteristics inherent to ASDs as the professionals attempted to determine which, if any, applied to their daughter. In order to differentiate the many ASDs, professionals must understand the diagnostic criteria that define each of the five ASDs. It is also essential for parents to fully understand the behavioral symptoms that are inherent to the diagnosis of an ASD so that they can better understand how their child has obtained this label and what this means for her future. In this chapter, we will review in detail typical behaviors of children with ASDs, focusing specifically on how these behaviors match up with diagnostic criteria and information included in the American Psychiatric Association's *Diagnostic and Statistical Manual of Mental Disorders,* Fourth Edition, more commonly known as the DSM-IV.

The DSM-IV, published in 1994, is a comprehensive review of diagnoses that fit under the umbrella of developmental or mental health disorders. It spells out behavioral characteristics that must be present to conclude a child has an ASD. To make a diagnosis, a professional evaluator compares a child's developmental history and behavioral profile with the behaviors listed under the various subcategories of ASDs in the DSM-IV.

Why are ASDs so Difficult to Diagnose?

There is wide room for interpretation when diagnosing ASDs. Unfortunately, there are no medical tests (e.g., a blood test), that can rule *in* or rule *out* the presence of an autism spectrum disorder. Because there is no definitive way to determine if a child has an ASD, a certain amount of unavoidable subjectivity is involved in diagnosing these children. Doctors must rely on observation, experience, a child's history, and their own good judgment. Given that there are five types of ASDs, diagnosis can get very complicated. A diagnosis of an ASD is determined solely by assessing whether or not a person demonstrates specific behaviors that fit within a diagnostic framework. In the United States, most doctors rely on criteria listed in the DSM-IV to make these diagnoses. Although the diagnostician may also use other assessment tools (see Chapter seven), the DSM-IV is acknowledged as the fundamental framework within which the possibility of an ASD is reviewed.

It should be noted that the general term for ASDs used in the DSM-IV is "pervasive developmental disorders," or PDDs. More recently, many professionals in the field have adopted the phrase "autism spectrum disorders" to replace the term PDD, most likely because the general population is more familiar with the term "autism" as well as to illustrate that there is a wide range of abilities (or "spectrum" of skills) among people with ASDs. For all practical purposes, the phrases are interchangeable.

Until the DSM-IV was published in 1994, there were only two subcategories of ASDs: Infantile Autism and Atypical Autism (now termed pervasive developmental disorder-not otherwise specified, or PDD-NOS). Therefore, the other three autism spectrum disorders (Asperger's disorder, Rett's disorder, and childhood disintegrative disorder) were rarely considered when professionals were evaluating children with unusual developmental patterns prior to 1994. If they were considered, it was because the diagnosticians were looking beyond the information available in the DSM. The inclusion of these other types of ASDs has caused quite a bit of confusion for parents and professionals when it comes to diagnosis. It has also broadened the number of children who fall within the diagnostic criteria, which may explain, in part, the rapid increase in the incidence of ASDs over the past few years.

Further complicating the diagnostic process, children with ASDs display a wide range of characteristics and abilities. There is no clear picture of a "typical" child with an ASD. One child with an ASD may be completely nonverbal and show little awareness of others, such as Kate Vance; another child may have an extensive vocabulary and show some degree of affection toward her family members.

It is important to note that all ASDs involve a "pervasive developmental disorder"; that is, the child's development is *disordered,* or shows an unusual pattern of skill acquisition **both within and between skill areas**. An example of disordered development *within* a skill area would be a child who can repeat verbatim an entire videotape but cannot carry on a simple conversation. That is, although language acquisition and vocabulary are well developed, the child does not understand the social use of language. An example of disordered development *between* skill areas is evident in a child, aged three, who has advanced fine motor skills (e.g., putting puzzles together), but does not seem to recognize her own parents. Disordered development can be very confusing and frustrating for parents. They may wonder, "If she can do *this,* why can't she do *that*?" Parents may also question if their child's unusual patterns of development are due to skill deficits or noncompliance. Having a "disordered development" is indicative of the diagnosis, and therefore the presence of it makes it easier to determine that an ASD is present.

The "Triad of Symptoms"

There are three major areas of concern for all children with autism spectrum disorders, sometimes referred to as a "triad" of symptoms: qualitative impairments in social skills; qualitative impairments in communication; and the presence of ritualistic, repetitive activities and interests. That is, the child shows unusual behaviors during social interactions, atypical communication, and demonstrates odd behaviors that may be repeated over and over again. (More details and examples of each of these characteristics are provided later in this chapter.) Regardless of the autism spectrum disorder that is diagnosed, the child will show the above three characteristics to some degree. Also, these behavioral criteria must be exhibited prior to three years of age.

The Triad of Symptoms for ASDs

1. Qualitative impairments in social skills
2. Qualitative impairments in communication
3. Presence of ritualistic, repetitive activities and interests

Presently, there are five subgroups of pervasive developmental disorders included in the DSM-IV: autistic Disorder, Asperger's disorder, Rett's disorder, childhood disintegrative disorder (CDD), and pervasive developmental disorder-not otherwise specified (PDD-NOS). This chapter will review, in detail, the diagnostic criteria and behaviors associated with each of these conditions. A table listing each type of ASD with its diagnostic criteria abridged is provided as a quick reference in Chapter Six, *Pinpointing the Right ASD Diagnosis*.

A Review of the Diagnostic Criteria for Each Autism Spectrum Disorder

Please note that the bold-face text in the following section indicates information that is directly quoted with permission from the American Psychiatric Association's *Diagnostic and Statistical Manual of Mental Disorders*, Fourth Edition (DSM-IV).

I. Autistic Disorder

Autistic disorder is the most common autism spectrum disorder and the one most people are familiar with. The designation "autistic disorder" is synonymous with the word "autism" and was earlier referred to as Infantile autism or Kanner's syndrome. To avoid confusion, we will use the phrase "autistic disorder" throughout this book to refer to this one of the five ASDs. The incidence of autistic disorder has increased rapidly over the past ten years and is now cited to be approximately one in five hundred. There are four times as many boys as girls diagnosed with autistic disorder and most children diagnosed with this disorder live a full lifetime. The eventual prognosis for a child with autistic disorder is difficult to predict. The level of supervision required by adults with autistic disorder can range from minimal assistance to ongoing daily assistance. However, the majority of people diagnosed with autistic disorder require some type of assistance throughout their lives.

By definition, the symptoms of autistic disorder begin prior to three years of age. Early signs may include disinterest in snuggling as an infant or absence of initiating eye contact spontaneously or with prompting. Some research points to three early signs, detectable by age one, that increase the probability that autistic disorder is present: the absence of 1) looking at others' faces, 2) responding to one's name, and 3) pointing (Osterling & Dawson, 1994).

Infants and babies with autistic disorder often seem disinterested or unaware of others in their environment. Parents may marvel at what an "easy" baby they have, without the typical infant demands such as crying to be held or entertained by others. However, a baby with autistic disorder may be highly upset by changes in the environment or routine, diapering, or bathing. She may stare at bright lights or spinning objects for prolonged periods of time. Kate Vance's preoccupation with staring at reflective surfaces is an example of this type of behavior. Because of her inability to imitate social actions, a very young child with autistic disorder may not catch on to early social games such as "peek-a-boo."

Most parents turn a blind eye to the somewhat unusual early development of their infant, but become more concerned when their child's language development does not develop as expected around the age of two. Some children develop speech and use a small vocabulary, then unexpectedly and for no apparent reason lose it. This delay or drop off in expressive speech is usually the first sign that parents notice and respond to by seeking professional assistance. In addition, many young children with autistic disorder don't respond to other people speaking to them, by either turning to look at them, gesturing, or verbalizing a response. For this reason, the first step many parents take is to have their child's hearing tested. More often than not, hearing is found to be within the normal range. Once this concern is ruled out, parents focus on helping their child learn to use language and often pursue some type of formal speech and language evaluation. It is not uncommon for a child with autistic disorder to be two, three, or even four years old before a professional evaluation occurs.

Diagnostic Criteria for Autistic Disorder

The American Psychiatric Association's *Diagnostic and Statistical Manual*, Fourth Edition (DSM-IV) lists the following diagnostic criteria for autistic disorder, previously known as Infantile Autism or "Kanner's Syndrome." Note that the triad of concerns discussed earlier is present: Qualitative impairments in social skills, qualitative impairments in communication, and the presence of restricted and repetitive behaviors.

A child does not have to demonstrate all of the diagnostic criteria listed below to be labeled with autistic disorder. However, she must demonstrate a total of at least six symptoms within these categories, with at least two being in the area of qualitative impairment in social skills, at least one in the area of qualitative impairment in communication, and at least one in the area of restricted and repetitive behaviors. Each symptom observed has to have been seen frequently in order to be "counted" when ascertaining if autistic disorder is present.

1. Qualitative impairment in social interaction, as manifested by at least two of the following:

- **Marked impairment in the use of multiple nonverbal behaviors such as eye-to-eye gaze, facial expression, body postures, and gestures to regulate social interaction.** Although absence of eye contact has probably been exaggerated as an essential characteristic of autistic disorder, it is certainly a common occurrence in children and adults. Other behavioral examples within this category include absence of snuggling, a "flat affect" (i.e., facial expression that is unchanging and unanimated during social interactions), and the absence of using gestures to initiate interactions, such as holding arms up to indicate a wish to be picked up.

- **Failure to develop peer relationships appropriate to developmental level.** When evaluating a child, it is important to remember that strong peer relationships are not expected in typical development until a child is at least three or four years old. Younger children have little understanding of the characteristics of a good friendship. For example, a typically developing three year old may designate a new friend as a "best friend," but then be unable to tell you the new friend's name. Therefore, age is an important factor when determining if this particular characteristic is present.

    Children with autistic disorder may have very little interest in other children. Kate Vance's apparent disinterest in her sister is a typical example of this pattern. One mother lamented that her husband and older son had been away on a trip for a week and the child with autistic disorder did not appear to recognize their absence or notice their return. Children with autistic disorder tend to learn to initiate interactions with adults before peers because they have recognized that adults are more able to meet their basic needs for food, drink, and assistance.

- **A lack of spontaneous seeking to share enjoyment, interests, or achievements with other people (e.g., by a lack of showing, bringing, or pointing out objects of interest).** Children who are typically developing can be demanding in their wish for others to share in their interests, activities, or areas of enjoyment. Many parents feel exhausted after spending time with a toddler who repeats, "Look at this!" and "Watch me!" throughout the day. In contrast, children with autistic disorder are rarely motivated to share things of interest with others. More often, these children will initiate an interaction only to communicate an immediate, tangible need such as hunger, thirst, or assistance, rather than to share enjoyment.

- **Lack of social or emotional reciprocity.** "Social or emotional reciprocity" is a rather vague term and can cause much confusion for parents and professionals. In a nutshell, this phrase refers to the fact that people with autistic disorder show little ability to or perhaps interest in interacting with others. They are often described as "being in their own world." They may appear socially detached and unaware of what others are doing or feeling. Children with autistic disorder may smile, although not necessarily towards another person, when feeling pleasure. Parents may feel depressed when their child does not run to them upon their return from work or respond in a nurturing fashion when the parent cries. Some people have hypothesized that people with autistic disorder have an innate *in*ability to recognize that other people have personal feelings and needs (referred to as "Theory of Mind"). For this reason, children with autistic disorder (as well as the other ASDs) may not develop the ability to empathize with others without treatment.

2. **Qualitative impairments in communication as manifested by at least one of the following:**
   - **Delay in, or total lack of, the development of spoken language (not accompanied by an attempt to compensate through alternative modes of communication such as gestures or mime).** Approximately thirteen percent of individuals with autistic disorder never develop any speech. The majority of people with autistic disorder learn to communicate through speech, although their verbal skills are usually underdeveloped or less functional than those of their typically develop-

ing peers. Some children find it easier to communicate through signing, augmentative devices, picture communication systems, or a combination of these techniques. A small percentage of children with autistic disorder show a loss of speech; that is, they demonstrate initial signs of language development and then there is a regression and the child no longer verbalizes formerly acquired words.

It is important to note that the diagnostic criteria states alternative means of communicating such as gestures or mime are *not* evident in children with autistic disorder. Many children with speech delays make repeated attempts to communicate through facial expressions, pointing, idiosyncratic signs, or vocalizations. In contrast, children with autistic disorder appear much less motivated or able to communicate with others.

- **In individuals with adequate speech, marked impairment in the ability to initiate or sustain a conversation with others.** Many people with autistic disorder may learn to speak a wide variety of words and even have an impressive vocabulary. However, their ability to use language functionally, especially within a social context, is often limited. The typical "back and forth" of conversation does not come naturally to people with autistic disorder. For example, some children can recite long passages from books or videotapes but are unable to respond appropriately when asked simple social questions such as, "How are you?" or "What's your name?" Often, conversations that *do* occur follow the pattern of the child responding to a series of questions asked by an adult without the child asking any questions of her own.

  In addition, it is frequently difficult to teach children with autistic disorder to change the intonation of their speech according to the content of their message.

As a consequence, they will often use a monotone, "robot-like" voice or speak in an unusual manner, such as whispering regardless of any need to be quiet.

■ **Stereotyped and repetitive use of language or idiosyncratic language.** Certain unusual language characteristics are often seen in children with autistic disorder. Some children repeat what they have just heard, called echolalia, either immediately or some time afterwards. In one classroom, the teachers never had to watch the weather on the evening news because one little boy would repeat verbatim the weather report during the next school day. It is not uncommon for toddlers who are typically developing to repeat what they hear as they are attempting to process information; therefore, echolalia in very young children is not particularly concerning. However, when echolalia is evident in children aged three or older, the possibility of autistic disorder may begin to be questioned.

Another language peculiarity sometimes seen in children with autistic disorder is "pronominal (refers to pronoun) reversal." This happens when a child refers to herself in the third person rather than using the word "I." For example, "Peter wants a cookie" rather than "I want a cookie." In the past, this tendency was interpreted as an indication that the child had no "sense of self" or identity. Nowadays, professionals recognize this tendency is due to a child's overall cognitive deficits. Recognizing that the words "I" and "you" are situation-specific requires abstract thinking that many children with autistic disorder lack. Over time, many children with autistic disorder begin to understand the concept of pronouns and when to use them appropriately.

Some people with autistic disorder develop their own idiosyncratic words or phrases to communicate. For example, one boy repeated the phrase "One, two, three, four, five…Ding!" whenever he became agitated. At first, his verbalizations were confusing until it was discovered that his parents gave him a five-minute "Time Out" for challenging behavior. They would set a timer to indicate when the "Time Out" was over. Eventually the phrase "One, two, three, four, five…Ding!" was interpreted to mean, "I had better calm down or my parents will put me in Time Out!" Although unusual on the surface, his methods were quite effective in calming himself.

Due to their limited language, some children with autistic disorder may repeat peculiar phrases that seem out of context but are in fact communicating their wish to initiate a social interaction. One girl would often say, "Play with string?" when in fact she had no interest in playing with string but was seeking social interaction. Many children are unable to say typical opening comments such as, "How are you?" or "Let's play" unless formally taught to do so. At other times, children with autistic disorder will repeat certain phrases merely because they like the sound or the sensory feedback they receive from producing the sounds. For example, a child may say the word "bubble" repeatedly because she enjoys the feeling it produces on her lips.

▪ **Lack of varied, spontaneous make-believe play or social imitative play appropriate to developmental level.** Although play is not a means of communication per se, this characteristic is included in this section because more sophisticated play involves communicating within a social context. Most children with autistic disorder have a limited ability to play appropriately by themselves or with others. Although they are sometimes skilled at concrete, isolated play activities such as completing puzzles or stacking blocks, they rarely engage in the symbolic use of objects, or pretend play. They may line up toys in a stereotypic, or ritualistic manner, or spin objects. Often they don't understand how toys are supposed to be used but instead manipulate them in an unusual way (e.g., spinning the wheels of a toy car). They are often more interested in objects than toys, much to the dismay of many a parent on Christmas morning or at birthday parties. Imaginative play is a rare occurrence for most young children with autistic disorder; in fact, most play is rather repetitive and ritualistic. With intervention, many children eventually learn to enjoy using toys in traditional ways or to engage in more sophisticated play activities.

3. **Restricted repetitive and stereotyped patterns of behavior, interests, and activities, as manifested by at least one of the following:**

- **Encompassing preoccupation with one or more stereotyped and restricted patterns of interest that is abnormal either in intensity or focus.** Children with autistic disorder tend to become obsessed with one or two topics or objects. For example, a child may become overly attached to an object and insist that she have the object in hand at all times. Some of the more common items of interest for children include trains, letters, numbers, and dinosaurs. One boy was especially interested in construction cones and insisted on carrying one with him all day and sleeping with it at night! Another child enjoyed holding leaves and carried her collection of leaves in a backpack. A relatively adept young woman who had graduated from college and was living in a semi-independent apartment was overly focused on flags and Russia. She drew a picture of the Russian flag and slept with it every night. Her trip to Philadelphia was especially memorable after she drove down Benjamin Franklin Parkway, which is lined with the flags of the world.

- **Apparently inflexible adherence to specific, non-functional routines or rituals.** A number of people with autistic disorder engage in ritualized behaviors that seem to serve no clear purpose. One man always tapped the wall as he left a room and appeared to feel more secure after doing so. Some children insist that doors are kept either open or shut at all times. Some think these tendencies are similar to the rituals that people with obsessive-compulsive disorder (OCD) engage in. For people with OCD and those with autistic disorder, these behaviors promote a sense of calm or security. However, individuals with obsessive-compulsive disorder are aware that their rituals are in fact nonfunctional, whereas people with autistic disorder seem to be oblivious of this fact. Many parents have found themselves willing to tolerate or even participate in various unusual rituals just to maintain peace in their home.

  Another way this particular diagnostic criterium plays itself out is when a person with autistic disorder overreacts to changes in her routine or environment. It is not uncommon for people with autistic disorder to become highly upset over the slightest change, which professionals refer to as an "insistence on sameness." For example, one girl became inconsolable for days after her parents replaced the living room couch. Her parents spent many hours trying to determine the reasons for her tantrums because unfortunately she did not have the communication skills to explain why she was so upset. When they bought an exact replica of their old couch, their daughter's behavior improved immediately.

- **Stereotyped and repetitive motor mannerisms (e.g., hand or finger flapping or twisting, or complex whole body movements).** Many people with autistic disorder display repetitive actions such as hand-flapping or fingerplay (twisting, bending, or flicking fingers), especially when excited. The term used to describe these behaviors is "stereotyped" or "stereotypies." They may rock their bodies back and forth as a means of providing self-stimulation or calm. Toewalking (walking on one's toes as opposed to heel then toe) is not uncommon, even when there are no clear physical reasons. Some children engage in headweaving (rocking their heads from side to side), while others may twirl in place. Facial grimacing can also occur. Children often appear oblivious to their environment while engaged in these behaviors. The blanket term frequently used for these actions is "self-stimulatory behaviors."

For the most part, self-stimulatory behaviors appear to be motivated by the internal consequences they produce. In other words, a child finds them pleasurable because of the sensory input or sense of calm they provide. Many people hypothesize that even pain-inducing behaviors can be calming in function. Some professionals theorize that children with autistic disorder have difficulty understanding what the input from their five senses are telling them and therefore receive a different physical sensation when engaged in these behaviors as compared to typically developing children.

- **Persistent preoccupation with parts of objects.** Whereas a person with autistic disorder may be disinterested in an object as a whole, she may, at times, be particularly interested in specific aspects of that object. Some children scrutinize objects in an apparent attempt to study the particular parts of the object. For example, some children enjoy staring at or rubbing shiny surfaces, gazing at reflections, scrutinizing knobs or screws, or overfocusing on parts of a toy. Instead of noticing an entire object such as a picket fence, some children who enjoy the visual input produced by a strobe effect may spend hours running back and forth while gazing at a fence, producing a fast-paced visual pattern of light and dark. Many parents become concerned that this behavior may indicate or even create a visual impairment, but more than likely the children simply enjoy investigating things in detail and there is no reason to think that this behavior will cause a visual impairment.

II. Asperger's Disorder

Interestingly, at the same time that Leo Kanner was describing a group of children as "autistic," a Viennese physician, Hans Asperger, was studying a group of similarly developing children. Both Kanner and Asperger published reports in the early 1940s regarding their findings; however, they were unaware of each other's theories and Asperger's work was only recently translated into English. As mentioned earlier, Asperger's disorder was not even included in the American Psychiatric Association's diagnostic manual until its 1994 revision. As a consequence, many children who are now adolescents or adults with Asperger's disorder were either misdiagnosed or remained undiagnosed for years. Only now do we have the opportunity to better understand their condition. Misdiagnoses that were usually assigned to these children included Attention-Deficit/Hyperactivity Disorder (AD/HD), Mild Autism, or PDD-NOS. Young adults with Asperger's disorder describe their childhood as a time of confusion, when they recognized they were "different" than peers but unable to understand why.

Research regarding Asperger's disorder is limited. However, certain trends have been discovered. Similar to autistic disorder, Asperger's disorder is more common in boys than girls. Although Asperger's disorder is thought to be less common than autistic disorder, the actual incidence has yet to be determined.

As a general rule, the prognosis for a child with Asperger's disorder is more positive than for other ASDs because it doesn't include cognitive impairment as part of the diagnostic criteria. Although adults with Asperger's disorder may continue to show some idiosyncratic behaviors (e.g., social awkwardness or obsessions regarding a particular topic), they are often able to live on their own.

The major characteristics of Hans Asperger's group of children in the 1940s were significant difficulties with social interactions and communication even though typical language acquisition had occurred and the children had normal intellectual skills. These characteristics have held relatively true through the years and continue to be the hallmarks of Asperger's disorder. Due to the label's relative newness, at least within the United States, Asperger's disorder has been an especially confusing diagnosis for many professionals and parents. At times the term is used rather loosely and with little consideration of the specific diagnostic criteria required for this label.

More often than not, the diagnosis of Asperger's disorder is made when a child is six years or older as compared to children diagnosed early on with other ASDs. For children with Asperger's disorder, early developmental milestones usually occur within the normal framework, with the exception of motor development. Delays in the areas of small and large muscle movement are common and these children are sometimes considered rather uncoordinated. For example, a young child with Asperger's disorder may trip often or have difficulty playing on playground equipment. As you may recall, the first major "red flag" for parents of children with other autism spectrum disorders is usually the lack of language development. In children with Asperger's disorder, language acquisition tends to occur within the expected time frame, so parents are less apt to be concerned until the child is school-aged. At this point, school personnel may notice behavioral differences that the parents missed when the child was younger. However, in retrospect, parents often are able to identify certain peculiarities of *early* development.

Early signs of Asperger's disorder can include:
- limited interest in playing with peers,
- unusual use of language,
- unusual reasoning ability, i.e., lack of common sense and the tendency to interpret comments literally,
- excessive interest in a particular topic and memorization of facts regarding this topic,
- difficulty recognizing and responding appropriately to others' emotions, and
- an inability to follow the give-and-take of conversation.

Many children with Asperger's disorder are quite bright, especially in their ability to recite factual knowledge about their particular areas of interest. For example, one eight-year-old boy could recite the schedules of all the major train stations across the country. Intellectual abilities tend to be within the normal range if not above average, as compared to individuals with other types of ASDs, who frequently test in the mentally retarded range. As a consequence, the overall prognosis for children diagnosed with Asperger's disorder tends to be more promising.

Although a delay in communication is rare in children with Asperger's disorder, peculiarities in their *use* of language may be present. For example, a child may make comments without realizing that the listener cannot understand what she's talking about without more background information. For example, when asked what his computer screen name was, one teenager with Asperger's disorder replied, "Paphos." When asked why he had chosen this name, he scoffed, "It's a town in *Cyprus!*" in a tone that implied the reasoning should have been clear to the most casual of listeners. In addition, the language that people with Asperger's disorder use tends to include rather formal phrases or dialogue from a familiar movie, commercial, or video game. In contrast to people with other ASDs, who may repeat movie phrases out of context, children with Asperger's disorder often insert them in actual social situations that initially appear appropriate. For instance, one boy would respond, "I feel displaced and dispassionate" during peer interactions. His parents discovered in time that he was repeating a phrase from a favorite movie.

Diagnostic Criteria for Asperger's Disorder

In contrast to individuals with autistic disorder, people with Asperger's disorder tend to have average or above average intelligence and show typical language development. However, as you will see, the diagnostic criteria for Asperger's disorder are very similar to those listed for a diagnosis of autistic disorder. Consequently, it is not uncommon for a child to fit both sets of diagnostic criteria, prompting confusion for parents. Given the overlapping diagnostic criteria, it is possible that a child may be diagnosed with autistic disorder when young and then Asperger's disorder as she gains greater skills over the years. Because of this confusion between the two conditions, some professionals in the field propose they not be considered separate entities but rather different manifestations of the same disorder. If your child has been diagnosed with both autistic and Asperger's disorder, recognize that the particular diagnosis that is chosen is less important than the need to identify effective intervention strategies for your child.

The DSM-IV outlines the following diagnostic criteria for Asperger's disorder. A child does not have to demonstrate all of the diagnostic criteria listed below to be labeled with Asperger's disorder. However, she must demonstrate at least three symptoms within these categories, with at least two being in the area of qualitative impairment in social skills, and at least one in the area of restricted and repetitive behaviors. Each symptom observed has to have been seen frequently in order to be "counted" when ascertaining if Asperger's disorder is present.

1. **Qualitative impairment in social interaction, as manifested by at least two of the following:**
   - **Marked impairment in the use of multiple nonverbal behaviors such as eye-to-eye gaze, facial expression, body postures, and gestures to regulate social**

interaction. People with Asperger's disorder tend to have difficulty responding appropriately to social interactions. Eye contact is often either absent or involves staring at others. Their facial expressions can often be flat with little emotional response to others'. Children with Asperger's disorder often have difficulty responding to physical signs of affection such as hugging. They may stand too close or too far away from others.

- **Failure to develop peer relationships appropriate to developmental level.** As mentioned earlier, many people with Asperger's disorder show little interest in forming friendships with peers. They often don't express any concern or sadness about this since they are often more content to play on their own. At the same time, some children with Asperger's disorder are overly affectionate with peers to the point of causing uneasiness. Or they may interact with peers in a very rule-governed manner with inflexible expectations of how each person should act. Their interpersonal style tends to be rather stilted and they may use unusually formal phrases when speaking to peers. For example, one five-year-old boy often responded to peer play initiations by saying, "I'd rather not participate at the moment."

- **A lack of spontaneous seeking to share enjoyment, interests, or achievements with other people (e.g., by a lack of showing, bringing, or pointing out objects of interest to other people).** Not unlike people with autistic disorder, individuals with Asperger's disorder are often self-absorbed, especially when it comes to their specific areas of interest. Although they may choose to discuss their interests with others, it is usually done in a mechanical, rather than conversational, manner (e.g., listing a multitude of facts regarding roller coasters). These interactions tend to be rather one-sided, with the person with Asperger's disorder sharing information for their own pleasure, not that of the listener. In fact, a person with Asperger's disorder may appear disinterested in others' areas of interest and will typically return the topic to their own preoccupations.

■ **Lack of social or emotional reciprocity.** People with Asperger's disorder can have very little understanding of social customs, especially when it comes to others' emotions and needs. They may laugh when someone is crying or refrain from seeking comfort from others when they are sad. People with Asperger's disorder are usually unable to recognize and respond appropriately to subtle social cues such as someone looking at their watch to indicate they need to leave. Their interactions tend to be direct and at times blunt. People with Asperger's disorder may make comments that on the surface appear rude, but they are merely "stating the facts" without intending to be malicious. At times this lack of social or emotional reciprocity can result in a person with Asperger's disorder being repeatedly disciplined (especially before a diagnosis has been determined), because her comments are misinterpreted or taken personally by others. Over time, many people with Asperger's disorder eventually learn to become attached to others in their lives.

2. **Restricted repetitive and stereotyped patterns of behavior, interests, and activities, as manifested by at least one of the following:**
    ■ **Encompassing preoccupation with one or more stereotyped and restricted patterns of interest that is abnormal either in intensity or focus.** One of the hallmarks of Asperger's disorder is intense focus on particular subjects, resulting in hours spent researching and discussing the topics. People with Asperger's disorder may

find it appealing to research and memorize a multitude of facts about relatively sophisticated subjects, such as geography or space exploration. For example, one adolescent with Asperger's disorder has a passion for the movie "Gone With The Wind" and will spend hours watching the movie and interpreting its meaning.

It is often unclear why a particular subject is chosen as the individual's preoccupation. As one man stated, "I didn't pick my passion; it chose *me.*" Interestingly, these preoccupations tend to share certain characteristics. First, the topics usually allow for the rote memorization of lists or characteristics, or categorizing into subsets. Second, they involve relatively sophisticated, rather than commonly known, facts. And, finally, they can be studied without any social input or obligation, by means of reading, searching the Internet, or watching television documentaries.

Older children and adults with Asperger's disorder usually come to recognize these preoccupations can be dysfunctional and will take deliberate steps to control their thoughts and actions, much the same way an individual with obsessive-compulsive disorder can use these techniques to control compulsions.

- **Apparently inflexible adherence to specific, nonfunctional routines or rituals.** People with Asperger's disorder sometimes insist upon engaging in rituals that can be quite complicated or time-consuming. Often, the rituals are related to their area of preoccupation. For example, a youngster with Asperger's disorder, who is fascinated with dinosaurs, insists her plastic dinosaurs be placed in a sophisticated pattern every morning before the school bus arrives. Many a morning the bus will wait outside her house as her parents try to hurry her along with this ritual. Although these rituals can be time-consuming and difficult for parents, there are interventions, such as Social Stories (see Chapter Nine), that can help children become less ritualistic.

- **Stereotyped and repetitive motor mannerisms (e.g., hand or finger flapping or twisting, or complex whole body movements).** In contrast to the repetitive body movements seen in people with other ASDs, such as rocking or flipping objects in a repetitive fashion, the behaviors seen in people with Asperger's disorder tend to be more subtle and less obtrusive. This may be because people with Asperger's disorder are a bit more cognizant of social norms and expectations. Examples of repetitive movements that people with Asperger's disorder may engage in include twirling one's hair or rubbing one's thumb to the point of creating a callous.

- **Persistent preoccupation with parts of objects.** Although some people with Asperger's disorder are preoccupied with parts of objects, this tendency is generally less intense than for people with autistic disorder. One child finds storm pipes with a ninety degree angle especially interesting and can name the location of each of these pipes within a five mile radius of her house. Another child is especially focused on the letters imprinted in stone bridges and insists that her mother stop the car for a minute or so whenever they cross bridges with these insignias.

III. Childhood Disintegrative Disorder (CDD)

Childhood disintegrative disorder (CDD) is a very rare disorder (approximately 5 in every 10,000 births) that is also called "Late Onset Autistic Disorder, " "Heller's Syndrome," and "Dementia Infantilis." Most children with CDD are boys, although the actual male:female ratio is unknown. First described in the early 1900s by special educator Theodore Heller in Vienna, the developmental history of children with this condition is characterized by typical development for at least the first two years of life. However, a notable regression then occurs. Developmental areas that are usually affected include social skills, bowel or bladder control, motor skills, communication, play skills, interpersonal interactions, and the use of nonverbal behaviors, such as gestures and facial expressions to communicate. Children with CDD may show an increase in challenging behaviors, such as physical aggression against others, or tantrums. Some children may have difficulty awakening from sleep.

Developmental deterioration can occur over a period of weeks or months. This regression typically occurs when the child is between the ages of two and four; however, this diagnosis can be warranted if regression occurs up until age ten. Sometimes there are preliminary behavioral changes prior to the regression such as increased irritability, heightened activity levels, or anxiety. The pattern of regression across various skill areas may be different. For example, a child may first begin to lose speech and later show regression in bowel or bladder control.

Ultimately, a child with CDD displays delayed development in at least two of the three areas affected in other ASDs; that is, qualitative impairments in social functioning, qualitative impairments in communication, and the presence of restricted or repetitive patterns of behavior or interest. Sadly, childhood disintegrative disorder usually overlaps with severe mental retardation and the overall prognosis for children with this disorder tends to be quite poor. Children are typically quite severely limited in their skills across all developmental areas, especially in the areas of communication and interpersonal interactions. As a consequence, special education services and support are almost invariably required for the remainder of the person's life. The lifespan for individuals with CDD is apparently the same as the general population. Fortunately, regression in skills usually tapers off and children with CDD are able to acquire some new skills over time.

Rest assured, the term "disintegrative" does not mean that the regression will continue indefinitely or that the deterioration ends in death. As mentioned earlier, a plateau tends to occur, after which your child usually begins to show slow progress. It is always important to rule out any possible physical cause for the regression in skills, such as infantile dementia (e.g., due to head trauma) or brain tumor. If the plateau seen in CDD does not occur, it is likely that there is a different cause for your child's deterioration of skills.

Although the actual cause(s) are not yet known, there appears to be a greater incidence of abnormal EEGs among children with CDD, as well as a higher frequency of seizure activity (especially during adolescence). This suggests that the central nervous system may play some role. Some researchers hypothesize there may be a predisposing genetic factor that, when combined with environmental stressors, results in the eventual regression of skills. These environmental factors might include viruses, birth trauma, toxin exposure, and prematurity. Other factors that may predispose a particular child to childhood disintegrative disorder include possible chromosomal abnormalities, a family history of autistic or Asperger's disorder, the presence of an autoimmune disorder, allergies, or asthma.

Due to the limited number of people with CDD, little is known about the condition and how best to treat it. However, most of the educational and behavioral treatment strategies used with people with autistic disorder will most likely help people with childhood disintegrative disorder as well. So far, no medications have proven effective in stopping the regression in skills. However, doctors may recommend medications to address some of the symptoms of CDD, such as hyperactivity or mood swings.

For parents of children with childhood disintegrative disorder, the drastic changes in your child are shocking and frightening. It is understandably difficult to comprehend how your child, who not long ago was playing excitedly, is now silently staring into space. You may respond to this situation by watching old videotapes or looking at photographs of your child before the regression began. Such responses, though understandable, are often heart-wrenching and ultimately unhealthy. It is more helpful to seek supportive therapy so you can begin the process of adjusting to your child's new future. Undoubtedly, this is easier said than done.

Diagnostic Criteria for Childhood Disintegrative Disorder

The DSM-IV outlines the following diagnostic criteria for child-hood disintegrative disorder. A child does not have to demonstrate all of the diagnostic criteria listed below to be labeled with CDD. However, she must demonstrate apparently normal development for the first two years of life, and at least two symptoms in each of the two subsequent categories. Each symptom observed has to have been seen frequently in order to be "counted" when ascertaining if CDD is present.

1. Apparently normal development for at least the first 2 years after birth as manifested by the presence of age-appropriate verbal and nonverbal communication, social relationships, play, and adaptive behavior. That is, the child's development appears to be right on track for the first two years or so of life. She is starting to speak, enjoys social interactions, and shows many of the typical developmental milestones reviewed in Chapter Two.

2. Clinically significant loss of previously acquired skills (before age 10 years) in at least two of the following areas:

- **Expressive or receptive language** (i.e., ability to speak as well as understand what is said). For example, the child may have a vocabulary of quite a few words and then lose the ability to say these words. Or, the child was able to understand simple directions but now is unable to respond.

- **Social skills or adaptive behavior** (i.e., ability to perform daily living skills such as dressing, eating, bathing, etc.). For instance, the child was able to eat using a spoon or fork but now only eats finger foods.

- **Bowel or bladder control.** Perhaps the child was formerly toilet trained but is now having frequent accidents.

■ **Play** (e.g., ability to play appropriately with toys). For example, a child who was able to build simple structures with blocks but now merely throws or drops the blocks.

■ **Motor skills** (e.g., loss of mobility, loss of coordination). A child may have been coordinated and walking easily but is now falling frequently.

3. **Abnormalities of functioning in at least two of the following areas:**
   ■ **Qualitative impairment in social interaction (e.g., impairment in nonverbal behaviors, failure to develop peer relationships, lack of social or emotional reciprocity).**

   ■ **Qualitative impairments in communication (e.g., delay or lack of spoken language, inability to initiate or sustain a conversation, stereotyped and repetitive use of language, lack of varied make-believe play).**

   ■ **Restricted, repetitive, and stereotyped patterns of behavior, interests, and activities, including motor stereotypies and mannerisms** (e.g., similar to those exhibited by children with autistic disorder, described earlier).

   (Please refer to the diagnostic criteria for Autistic Disorder for a more detailed description of the above three categories of behaviors.)

Childhood disintegrative disorder is a devastating condition in many ways. However, remember that the incidence is very low and therefore it is highly unlikely your child has this disorder. Also, keep in mind that all children go through phases where they may show some regression in skills, so do not assume that CDD is present unless a qualified team of professionals has made this determination.

IV. Rett's Disorder

Rett's disorder was first identified by Austrian physician, Andreas Rett, in 1966. He described a small group of girls whose development as infants appeared only mildly delayed, if not typical. However, by the age of eighteen months, these young girls had shown a progressive loss of skill in the areas of manual, social, language, and gross motor development.

In contrast to the other autism spectrum disorders, which occur more commonly in males, Rett's disorder occurs almost exclusively in females. The prevalence is rather low and is cited as approximately 1 in 15,000 births. However, it is one of the leading causes of mental retardation in girls. It has been reported in all races and ethnic groups. Most children are diagnosed before the age of three or four and the condition persists throughout their lifetime.

In children with this rare form of autism spectrum disorder, the growth of the head circumference slows between five and forty-eight months of age. The development of the brain plateaus and difficulties with gait and balance result, as well as poor coordination in body movements in general ("ataxia"). Children who were previously walking unhindered may now have difficulty walking without falling. Overall muscle control becomes quite limited. For example, a child may start having difficulty holding onto objects or be unable to pick up small items.

One of the most common and easily identifiable behaviors inherent to Rett's disorder is repetitive hand-wringing while holding the hands at waist level. Children with Rett's disorder often do this for prolonged periods of time and will resist prompts to stop and perform different activities with their hands. Other unusual behaviors such as hyperventilating, facial grimacing, teeth grinding, or holding their breath may also occur. It's unclear why children with Rett's disorder do these things. One girl would hold her breath up to 289 times per day and actually faint sometimes as a consequence. Self-injurious behaviors, such as self-biting, can occur, as can excessive irritability.

The Four Phases of Rett's Disorder

Professionals in the field have outlined four separate phases of Rett's disorder:

- In **Stage I**, the infant develops relatively normally up until approximately twelve to eighteen months old but then shows a decreased interest in her surroundings (e.g., she may seem less alert or aware of other people). Head growth begins to slow down during this phase.

- **Stage II**, when the child is aged three to four years old, is characterized by a clear loss of previously acquired skills (especially communication), irritability, onset of hand-wringing, insomnia, and developmental delays, especially in the areas of social and language skills. The child often starts to experience seizures at this time.

- **Stage III** usually takes place approximately one year later, when the child is four or five, and involves some improvement in communication. During this phase, children with Rett's disorder are usually more sociable and even-tempered. However, there is a greater possibility of weight loss, hyperventilation, sleep apnea, and rigidity in motor coordination seen as stiff, robotic movements. Scoliosis (curvature of the spine) may develop during this time.

- **Stage IV**, which children reach at various ages, can last for the remainder of the person's life. During this phase, motor skills deteriorate, muscle tone is lost, and there can be an increase in spastic movements, all of which can result in the need to use a wheelchair. Seizure activity tends to wane during this final stage.

Research studies have brought to light clear differences in the brains of children with Rett's disorder as compared to those of children who are typically developing. Some studies have indicated that the brains of children with Rett's disorder are thirty percent smaller than average. It has also been discovered that there is a genetic component to Rett's disorder. In fact, Rett's disorder seems to be caused by a particular gene called "MeCP2" (Webb & Latif, 2001). Interestingly, when this particular gene was changed in mice so that their genetic makeup was similar to that seen in children with Rett's disorder, the mice showed the same unusual growth in head circumference as well as a tendency to wring their front paws together.

It is not uncommon for people with Rett's disorder to suffer from various medical conditions. Seizures can occur when a child is still under five years of age. In fact, seizures occur in seventy-five percent of children with Rett's disorder and can be particularly severe initially until medications are used to control them. Research indicates that children with Rett's disorder have a higher incidence of eating/digestive problems such as weight loss, chronic constipation, gastrointestinal reflux difficulties, difficulties chewing and swallowing, and calcium deficiencies. They may have sleep disturbances, awakening frequently in the middle of the night screaming or laughing with unknown cause. Adolescents or adults with Rett's disorder may sleep during the daytime and have difficulty getting to sleep at night. Also, scoliosis in people with Rett's disorder is common. Cardiorespiratory failure can occur. Medical interventions are more common for kids with Rett's disorder because of their special health concerns. Needless to say, parents of children with Rett's disorder need to become "experts" in various medical concerns and interventions. The support of family and friends is essential due to the pressures inherent in having a child with Rett's disorder.

Children with Rett's disorder can benefit from the same educational and behavioral treatment strategies generally recommended for children with other ASDs. A child with Rett's disorder may have very limited speech and only understand short sentences and therefore it would be beneficial to add speech therapy to her educational plan. She will usually have poor gross and fine motor skills and may require occupational therapy services as well. The behavioral techniques discussed in Chapter Nine are often advantageous when developing a comprehensive treatment plan for children with Rett's disorder.

It is often very difficult to redirect a child with Rett's disorder when they are hand-wringing or displaying other repetitive movements, thus hindering teaching efforts. As a consequence of all of these concerns, learning is frequently slow and overall progress is limited. At the same time, these children *do* tend to eventually show improved interest in social interactions, which can be helpful in promoting overall learning and quality of life.

When comparing Rett's disorder with the other four ASDs, it is important to point out that it is the only condition that has clear and consistent *physical* signs (i.e., decelerated head growth, specific genetic differences). Although it is rare, it is the easiest ASD to differentiate during a diagnostic evaluation.

Diagnostic Criteria for Rett's Disorder

*The DSM-IV outlines the following diagnostic criteria for Rett's disorder. A child must demonstrate **all** of the diagnostic criteria listed below to be labeled with Rett's disorder. Each symptom observed has to have been seen frequently in order to be "counted" when ascertaining if Rett's disorder is present.*

1. All of the following:
   - **Apparently normal prenatal and perinatal development** (i.e., no signs of problems during pregnancy or in early infancy).

   - **Apparently normal psychomotor development through the first 5 months after birth** (i.e., the child was able to roll over independently and perhaps could sit up unassisted).

   - **Normal head circumference** (size) **at birth.**

2. Onset of all of the following after the period of normal development:

- **Deceleration of head growth between ages 5 and 48 months** (i.e., the growth of her head size slows down during this time).

- **Loss of previously acquired purposeful hand skills between ages 5 and 30 months with the subsequent development of stereotyped hand movements (e.g., hand-wringing or hand washing)** (e.g., the child may have been holding a rattle easily but now drops any object and wrings her hands continuously).

- **Loss of social engagement early in the course (although often social interaction develops later)** (e.g., the child may have smiled in response to other people's interaction but begins to be unresponsive to social initiations by others).

- **Appearance of poorly coordinated gait or trunk (whole body) movements** (e.g., awkward when walking, unable to jump in place).

- **Severely impaired expressive and receptive language development with severe psychomotor retardation** (e.g., difficulty speaking and understanding what is said to her).

V. Pervasive Developmental Disorder-Not Otherwise Specified (PDD-NOS)

Of all the autism spectrum disorders, PDD-NOS is the one that has created the most confusion for professionals and parents when it comes to zeroing in on an appropriate diagnosis. In contrast to the rather detailed diagnostic criteria outlined by the DSM-IV for the other ASDs, PDD-NOS is described with one brief paragraph:

> **This category should be used when there is a severe and pervasive impairment in the development of reciprocal social interaction or verbal and nonverbal communication skills, or when stereotyped behavior, interests, and activities are present, but the criteria are not met for a specific Pervasive Developmental Disorder...** (pp. 77-78)

What does this description really mean? First, "NOS," or "Not Otherwise Specified," categories in the DSM-IV pertain to individuals who show *some* of the requirements for a given diagnostic category, but whose overall symptoms are insufficient in intensity to warrant that particular diagnosis. Therefore, PDD-NOS is a diagnosis appropriate for people who have *some* of the qualities inherent in the general diagnostic category of "pervasive developmental disorders," but do not neatly fit into autistic disorder, Asperger's disorder, Rett's disorder, or childhood disintegrative disorder.

Regrettably, no clear guidelines are provided as to where to draw the diagnostic line when determining whether or not a child has PDD-NOS versus a mild form of autistic disorder or Asperger's disorder. As a consequence, every professional needs to develop her own subjective strategy for differentiating these conditions. These personal diagnostic judgments make for disagreement among professionals. It's not uncommon for the same child to be given the label PDD-NOS, Asperger's disorder, or "high functioning autism," depending upon the particular professional who is conducting the diagnostic evaluation.

Some parents see a diagnosis of PDD-NOS as an indication that their child is less affected than a child with autistic disorder or Asperger's disorder. By definition, this could, in fact, be true. However, it is important to point out that what one particular professional has determined is PDD-NOS according to *her own individualized decision-making process* may not be consistent with another evaluator's diagnosis. Diagnostic labels do not always stick and your child may receive a different diagnosis some time later. Furthermore, it is not uncommon for professionals to be wary about diagnosing a very young child as having autistic disorder and may use the PDD-NOS label as a way of gradually introducing the family to the world of autism spectrum disorders. While generous in its intent, this tendency only causes more confusion if a different diagnosis is more appropriate.

What should you do if your child receives more than one ASD diagnosis or if you disagree with the particular ASD diagnosis that is given? Keep in mind that there is quite a bit of subjectivity within the diagnostic criteria for the ASDs and therefore the different ASD labels provided to your child merely reflect the different opinions of the professionals involved. As will be discussed in Chapter Seven, the most important priority is to find a knowledgeable, experienced team of diagnosticians so that the eventual diagnosis that is identified is as accurate as possible.

"High-Functioning" Versus "Low-Functioning" Autism

It is not uncommon for professionals to use the terms "high-functioning" or "low-functioning" when describing children with autistic disorder. It is important for parents to recognize that there are no clear criteria used to make these determinations. Rather, these terms are used according to each professional's subjective perceptions. However, as a general rule, whether or not a child is deemed "high" or "low" functioning is usually related to 1) the presence or absence of mental retardation, 2) whether or not the child is verbal, and 3) the degree to which challenging behaviors are present. In other words, if a child has an IQ within the average range, can speak in short sentences, and is relatively cooperative, she may be described as "high functioning." In contrast, if a child has mental retardation, minimal speech, and exhibits significant problematic behaviors, it is more likely the term "low-functioning" will be used. These are merely guidelines so you can better understand how these terms may be used. If your child falls in between these descriptions, then the phrases "low" or "high" functioning will probably not be used. As parents, it is best to concentrate on your child's individualized strengths, weaknesses, and treatment needs rather than dwelling on these terms.

Concluding Remarks about Diagnostic Criteria

Hopefully the information in this chapter, as well as in Chapter Six, will provide the framework for a better understanding of how ASDs are diagnosed. The diagnostic criteria for each of the five ASDs can be confusing and difficult to follow. Needless to say, the confusion regarding overlapping criteria as well as differences in professional judgments can be highly frustrating for parents. However, it is important for parents to understand how each of the labels is determined and how their child may exhibit the behaviors required for an ASD diagnosis. The particular diagnosis that a child receives may influence her eventual school placement, availability of services, and future prognosis. Therefore, it is essential that the eventual diagnostic decision be a valid one. More in-depth information about school placement and services is presented in Chapter Seven.

Parents Speak

Experiences with "professionals" were not the best. Our pediatrician wasn't convinced anything was wrong with our daughter and the specialist left us with even more questions and few coping strategies. We became more interested in searching for other parents who knew the ropes, rather than professional advice.

5 | Common Features of Autism Spectrum Disorders

The Williams Family

Nora and Ryan Williams were apprehensive as they entered the large community center on that crisp autumn evening. Their social worker had suggested they attend a parent group that met at the center each month so that parents of children with autism spectrum disorders could share insights, information, and support. Both Nora and Ryan were unsure what to expect since their son Harry was only four years old and had only recently been diagnosed with an ASD. As they entered the large room filled with parents, they were grateful to recognize one of the other parents, who escorted the Williamses to the babysitting room.

As they held little Harry's hand and looked around the room, their apprehension increased. Did Harry fit in with this group of children? Some of the children seemed oblivious to others, sitting on the floor and spinning toys in a repetitive fashion, while other children were actively seeking adult attention and seemed generally more adept.

Once Harry was settled, Nora and Ryan joined the rest of the parents at the meeting. As the parents discussed their thoughts and concerns, the Williamses were struck by the fact that no two stories were exactly alike. In fact, there were moments when the children described sounded very little like Harry. It dawned on Nora as she listened to the other parents that children with ASDs, just like all children, are diverse in their abilities and needs.

At the same time, there were common themes which bound the parents' experiences: The frustration they experienced when they *found it difficult to "reach" their child and the wish that their child could communicate more effectively. These shared experiences were expected considering that they were linked to the primary concerns in an individual with an ASD. However, Nora and Ryan were also surprised when they found out that many of the children shared other characteristics that were not commonly thought of when describing someone with an autism spectrum disorder.*

*Like Harry, quite a few of the children were drawn to letters and numbers. In fact, some of the younger children had already taught themselves to read! Many parents also described their child as being especially sensitive to certain noises such as the vacuum or a hairdryer. The Williamses could certainly relate to these descriptions since Harry would tantrum loudly whenever he heard these types of sounds. One couple reported that their son became very anxious when the seasons changed and insisted on wearing long-sleeves well into the first month of summer. By the time he adapted to wearing short-sleeves and shorts, fall arrived and everyone had to tolerate another transition period as he became reaccustomed to wearing long-sleeves and pants again. Ryan whispered to Nora, "Maybe **that** explains why Harry keeps hiding his long-sleeved shirts!" As they left the community center that night, Ryan and Nora realized they now had a fuller understanding of the condition known as autism spectrum disorder and the ways children with it are alike.*

Of course, no two people with autism spectrum disorders are exactly alike. In fact, a child could be diagnosed with an ASD without showing any of the following "common features." However, people with ASDs *tend* to share certain characteristics. **The characteristics listed in this chapter are not required for a diagnosis, but are rather features that are often present.** When determining whether a person has an autism spectrum disorder, a professional first and foremost reviews the diagnostic criteria listed in the DSM-IV. However, in addition to the diagnostic criteria outlined in the DSM-IV, the professional may be on the lookout for other characteristics often associated with an ASD. When many of the following characteristics are present, this may give the experienced professional an even clearer picture as to whether or not an ASD is present.

Common Features of an ASD

Well-Developed Motor and Visual-Motor Integration Skills

Of all the developmental areas (e.g., speech, social, self-help skills, etc.), motor development is usually an area of relative skill for people with autism spectrum disorders. Motor skills are usually categorized into two general types: gross motor and fine motor abilities. Gross motor skills involve large body movements, such as walking, riding a bike, and throwing a baseball. Fine motor skills require more discrete movements, such as writing letters or picking up a small pebble. Children on the spectrum frequently enjoy and seek out gross motor play, such as rough-housing and climbing on playground equipment. Likewise, it is not unusual to hear that these children are unusually adept at putting puzzles together or playing computer games, skills that involve integrating visual input with fine motor movements. This type of activity is termed "visual-motor integration" because it requires the child to coordinate what he sees with the ways in which he moves. Overall motor coordination is often a strength that can be capitalized upon when teaching people with ASDs new skills. The only exception to this trend is a reported pattern of motor discoordination sometimes observed in people with Asperger's disorder, as they can be rather clumsy at times. Also, as described in Chapter Four, children with Rett's disorder often have very poor coordination. Although they retain some degree of clumsiness throughout their lifetime, in general these children may show improved motor coordination over time.

Mechanical Skills

People with ASDs sometimes amaze their parents with their mechanical skills. One mother was astounded to discover her three-year-old son had taken apart all their kitchen cabinets using a screwdriver. Fortunately, he had removed the cabinet doors carefully and was more than willing to help her replace the doors afterwards! Children with ASDs are often able to operate relatively sophisticated machines independently, such as VCRs or DVD players at a young age.

Special Interest in Letters or Numbers

Every so often, a child with autism spectrum disorders is able to read at an especially young age (termed "hyperlexia"). Parents may find their child spelling out the names of their favorite videotapes using plastic letters, even though this skill was never explicitly taught. This ability to read and generate words may be seen in children with an ASD as young as three or four years old. However, this ability to read doesn't necessarily mean the child can also comprehend what he's reading (e.g., he may read a "Don't walk" sign and then walk across a busy street.)

If a child can read, this can be quite helpful for teaching purposes, because written techniques such as Social Stories (described in Chapter Nine) can be used to help children better understand their world, once they fully comprehend the meaning of written words. Often, children with autism spectrum disorders are drawn to numbers or letters even if they cannot read. For example, they may enjoy looking at books, lining up letters, or insisting that their parents repeatedly write numbers over and over on a blackboard.

Rote Memory Skills

People with ASDs sometimes demonstrate remarkable rote memory skills. At times, parents even rely upon their child's memory skills when trying to recall specifics and events of the past. Some people with ASDs are able to repeat detailed lists, dates, or schedules. Often this information is stated in a repetitive manner without regard to purpose, and is purely for the child's own pleasure rather than to communicate the information to others. Or, the recitations of memorized facts may calm the child, by enabling him to "tune out" the environment. For example, one young man with an ASD recites aloud a particular bus route when he is becoming agitated, pretending that he is going from stop to stop as he makes sounds that simulate shifting gears.

Mental Retardation

According to recent studies, upwards of 70 percent of people with ASDs also have mental retardation. "Mental retardation" is an often misunderstood term and deserves appropriate explanation. A person is said to have mental retardation if he earns an IQ of 70 or below on a standardized intelligence test. Keep in mind that the great majority of people in the world have an IQ between 85 and 115, with an average of 100. Therefore, an IQ of 70 or below is significantly lower than would be expected in the general population. In addition to an IQ below 70, he must show significant deficits in his ability to perform activities of daily living, such as self-help skills, communication, home maintenance, and social skills. People with mental retardation have significant delays across a wide variety of areas and tend to require some degree of supervision and support throughout their lives. There are varying degrees of mental retardation, ranging from mild to severe/profound. The qualification depends on the degree a person's overall skills are delayed compared to others the same age who are unaffected by mental retardation.

Knowing the degree of cognitive impairment may be useful to professionals in deciding what type of autism spectrum disorder is present. For example, people with Asperger's disorder or PDD-NOS frequently have cognitive skills within the average to above average range. This is not the case for people with other autism spectrum disorders. In fact, children with childhood disintegrative disorder and Rett's disorder often function within the moderate or even severe range of mental retardation. That is, their IQ is often 50 or below. If a child has been diagnosed with both an ASD plus mental retardation, this means his development will likely be more encumbered than a child diagnosed with an ASD alone. The amount of supervision and educational support is typically increased for these children as their overall learning curve is slower.

One of the more difficult diagnoses to make is determining if an individual already diagnosed with severe or profound mental retardation also has autism. People with such significant cognitive deficits inherently have difficulty in the areas of social skills and communication. It is not uncommon for these individuals to engage in repetitive, self-stimulatory behaviors as well. Since these are the three primary areas of concern when diagnosing an ASD, a professional must be adept in teasing out which deficits are due to the severe/profound mental retardation versus what is likely related to a potential ASD. Therefore, definitively diagnosing a child with autism and mental retardation, although possible, is more difficult. More on mental retardation and ASDs will be discussed in Chapters Six and Seven.

As noted in Chapter Three, traditional IQ tests can be verbally and socially biased. Meaning, a person taking an IQ test must have relatively good social and language skills in order to perform well. For example, a person must understand and care about the social expectations inherent in the administration of an IQ test. Also, he must be able to understand the evaluator's verbal instructions and at times respond verbally as well. Although the majority of people with ASDs have cognitive abilities within the mentally retarded range, this bias makes it very difficult to gauge the *degree* of impairment. Considering that language and social skills are two major areas of difficulty for people with ASDs, it is likely that traditional IQ tests underestimate, at least slightly, a person's actual intellectual ability. This is especially true for young children, since IQ scores only become reliable once children are six years and older. Although these considerations need to be taken into account regarding the use of traditional IQ tests, the scores derived from these assessments can still be helpful in gaining a realistic portrayal of your child's strengths and weaknesses. Please see Chapter Seven for additional information regarding specific intellectual tests that may be used during a comprehensive evaluation.

What are the advantages of determining whether or not your child has mental retardation as well as an autism spectrum disorder? Most importantly, the additional diagnosis will yield a better understanding of your child's overall development and needs and inform the treatment choices you make. Also, the additional label may open up doors for funding sources that might otherwise be unavailable.

Odd Responses to Sensory Stimuli

All of us receive input from the environment, whether it be via sight, smell, touch, taste, or hearing. The ability to interpret this input and make sense of it is integral to efficient and successful learning. Unfortunately, some children with ASDs demonstrate an over- or under-response to sensory input. For example, a person with an ASD may seem oblivious to someone calling his name but become very upset when he hears certain sounds, such as mechanical noises (e.g., those produced by appliances). Similarly, fire drills at school can be especially agitating for a child with an ASD. One child found having a pair of earmuffs in his desk calmed him, knowing he could put them on the moment the fire drill began. These are examples of overreacting and underreacting to *auditory* input.

Children with ASDs may over- or under-respond to other types of sensory stimuli as well. About half of these children find tactile input, or physical touch, very disturbing. They may tantrum during daily tasks such as washing their hair or putting on shoes. They may actively avoid hugging or other forms of physical affection. At the same time, they may deliberately seek deep pressure input, such as crawling under a bean bag chair or the cushions on a couch to feel the weight press upon them. In response to this desire for deep pressure, Dr. Temple Grandin, an internationally respected speaker with autism, created what became known as the "squeeze machine." Once a person crawls into this contraption, deep but gentle pressure, regulated by the user, is provided on each side of the body. Although Dr. Grandin finds hugging others uncomfortable, she reports that being in her "squeeze machine" is very calming. Perhaps the ability to regulate the amount of pressure experienced is what appeals to Dr. Grandin and others with ASDs.

People with autism spectrum disorders sometimes also respond to visual input in an unusual manner. They may stare at their hands for prolonged periods of time or gaze at shiny materials or surfaces. They may hold items up very close to their eyes, even though they have no vision problems. Some people with ASDs inspect objects using their peripheral vision, or out of the corner of their eye, rather than looking directly at them.

Children with autism spectrum disorders sometimes explore their environment in unusual and unexpected ways. They may smell a person's hair upon first meeting him, or put objects into their mouths as a means to learn about them. Some children eat inedible objects, such as dirt or string, a phenomenon known as "pica."

Distractibility and High Activity Level

Many people with autism spectrum disorders are highly active and distractible. However, the level of distractibility can be very situation-specific. For example, a child with an ASD may find it difficult to pay attention to something beyond a few seconds, but later become over-focused on an object or video and appear transfixed for long periods of time. It is not uncommon for people with ASDs to also be diagnosed with Attention-Deficit/Hyperactivity Disorder (AD/HD). Fortunately, there are specific medications that can very successfully address excessive activity or distractibility. However, professionals should be certain a child truly meets all of the criteria for AD/HD before making a definitive diagnosis. Any misdiagnosis can lead to confusion regarding the child's treatment needs.

Mood Lability

All of us experience changes in moods. For the most part, these mood changes are influenced by life's circumstances, such as the death of a loved one, an irritating job, or the birth of a child. "Mood lability" is a phrase used to describe someone whose moods, seemingly not influenced by environmental experiences, change quickly. Parents frequently describe their child with an ASD as displaying periods when he is "moody," "irritable," or "upset for no apparent reason." He may be laughing one minute and then become physically aggressive the next, with no clear motive. It can be difficult to keep up with your child's ever-changing emotions. Although no one knows for sure why these swift changes in moods occur, they may be due to biochemical changes in the brain, the child being upset regarding sensory input or unexpected changes in the environment, or frustration regarding the inability to effectively communicate.

Self-Injurious Behaviors

A small group of people with autism spectrum disorders display self-injurious behaviors, such as biting their hands, pinching their skin, and banging their heads. Interestingly, research shows that girls injure themselves in different ways than boys. Boys tend to engage in head-banging or head-hitting. Once the head-banging or head-hitting has been extinguished through a behavior modification plan, boys tend to demonstrate no other forms of self-injury. However, females are more likely to bite themselves and will often come up with other means of self-injury once you have successfully eliminated the self-biting.

Many children with ASDs appear to have an unusually high tolerance for pain. Some appear to derive some form of physical pleasure or self-stimulation from the behavior, which some professionals hypothesize is linked to the rush of endorphins released during times of pain. Other times, people with ASDs may hurt themselves in order to escape an undesirable activity. Even when people with ASDs don't injure themselves, some seem barely aware of pain or discomfort. They may have little or no reaction to extreme hot or cold. When hurt, they may engage in repetitive behaviors, known as stereotypies, such as rocking in order to self-calm rather than going to a parent for comfort.

Insistence on Sameness

As mentioned earlier, it is often difficult for people with ASDs to tolerate change in their routine or environment. They may become inconsolable when furniture is rearranged or when transitioning from one activity to another. One set of parents was forced to engage in a highly ritualized bedtime routine involving singing in unison while their daughter wore a bandage on her left pinky. If this ritual was not carried out, their child would scream and kick well into the night. This "insistence on sameness" may result from a child's inability to interpret and predict daily occurrences, leading to undue anxiety. It's not surprising that children with ASDs may find highly predictable daily routines and environments less nerve-wracking. It is important to actively teach your child that life is filled with surprises and changes and learning to live with change is an important skill for every child. See Chapter Nine for ideas about how to help your child learn new, appropriate behaviors.

Limited Food Preferences

Many children with autism spectrum disorders are picky eaters, tolerating only certain foods and drinks. This may have something to do with texture, for example the way a mushy banana or pulpy orange juice feels in their mouth. Or it may be related to a child's poor muscle control when chewing or swallowing. They may also have unusual eating habits, which might include eating foods in a particular order, only at certain times of the day or night, or only in the presence of certain people. These problems tend to be more pronounced in children under six years of age and generally diminish as they grow older. As discussed above, many children find change intolerable so convincing your child to try new foods can seem nearly impossible.

Sleep Disturbances

A number of children with ASDs have problems related to sleep, such as difficulty falling asleep, awakening for long periods during the night, or requiring less sleep than average during a twenty-four-hour period. Although no one is certain why people with ASDs tend to have sleep problems, they may very well be related to differences in brain chemistry or unusual reactions to the environment. For example, one child with autistic disorder awoke several times during the night until his parents realized he found the feeling of cotton sheets discomforting. Once they put silk sheets on his bed, the boy slept comfortably through the night. Needless to say, many parents are exhausted because of these erratic sleep patterns as well as concerned their child may wander during the night. At times it is helpful to use prescription medication to enable a child to sleep through the night so everyone wakes well-rested.

Lack of Danger Awareness

Parents are understandably concerned when their child with an ASD shows minimal awareness of safety issues. This limited safety awareness may be linked to the child's inability to learn from his experiences or from verbal warnings. Children with ASDs have been known to climb out onto roofs or up the outside railings of open staircases. Traffic safety is often an area of concern when a child is young and might run into the street, unaware of the danger cars pose. Implementing preventive strategies such as locking doors, using strollers when out in the community, and putting mat alarms outside your child's bedroom are often your best choices, especially when your child is young.

Depression

Children of any age with ASDs sometimes show symptoms of depression, such as a flat facial expression, disinterest in previously preferred activities, and periods of crying. At times, depression reveals itself as an increase in challenging behaviors, such as physical aggression or irritability. More verbal teens or young adults may be able to express depression as an increased awareness of their own limitations, or feeling "different" compared to peers. Although this increased awareness of one's differences can contribute to depression, depression can also be linked to biochemical imbalances in the brain.

Seizures

Some individuals with autism spectrum disorders, especially those with mental retardation, experience at least one seizure in their lifetime. These can be serious, wherein the entire brain is affected, called generalized seizures. Or they can be more subtle staring spells, wherein the child may appear to be non-responsive to anything or anyone for a few seconds or even longer. A thorough evaluation of the brain, including an EEG (Electroencephalogram), is often helpful in determining whether or not seizures are actually occurring. If further testing indicates that seizures are happening, medication is often helpful.

Concluding Remarks about Common Features of ASDs

As described in detail in Chapter Four, the three major areas of developmental differences in individuals with autism spectrum disorders are:

1. qualitative impairments in social interactions,
2. qualitative impairments in communication, and
3. the presence of apparently nonfunctional rituals or repetitive behaviors.

That is, these children show unusual behaviors within their social relationships and in their ability to communicate effectively, plus they engage in repetitive behaviors such as rocking, handflapping, lining up objects, etc. Although the characteristics listed in this chapter are frequently seen in people with ASDs, remember, they are **not** necessary for a diagnosis of an autism spectrum disorder. However, if a diagnostician sees that a child shows behavioral symptoms within the three primary diagnostic areas, the presence of some of the associated features listed in this chapter serves to further support the diagnosis.

Parents Speak

When my daughter was born, Danny was thirteen months old and that's when his eye contact and babbling started to deteriorate. At first, I thought this was happening because he was jealous of her. I still feel silly for thinking that a thirteen-month-old could be jealous. If I had only known, I would have started interventions right away.

ᖰᖱ

By the time the boys were three years old, everyone would ask if they were talking yet. I always had a ready excuse for them. I felt so responsible. As time went on, I got more and more concerned about their slow development. I dreaded being asked if they were talking yet.

ᖰᖱ

The thought of having a child with special needs was so overwhelming that I tried my best to make her appear "normal." I focused on her strengths and tried to work on her weaknesses by myself. I decided to wait until her three-year-old "well visit" to talk to our pediatrician about my concerns.

⌒

We noticed he would repeat lines from videos and walk around in circles a lot. We were first-time parents, so we weren't sure if this was normal for little boys. I remember feeling afraid to bring this stuff up to a professional or any of my friends. I wanted to just "wait it out" to see if things got better.

6 | Pinpointing the Right ASD Diagnosis

The O'Malley Family

Caroline and Peter O'Malley are feeling very confused. Their concern began when their son, David, was two years old. He spent hours watching the same videotapes and showed little interest in his toys. He became very upset during daily activities such as bathing, changing his diaper, and eating meals. Although they tried to reason with him, he never seemed to understand their explanations. His behavior and development seemed very different than that of his older sister, Laura, but their pediatrician wrote off their concerns as unwarranted. Comments such as "Boys develop slower" and "He's not talking because Laura is talking for him" did little to alleviate their worry.

Finally, when David turned three, his parents took him to a specialist at a local hospital. After a comprehensive assessment, the specialist diagnosed David as having autistic disorder. Caroline and Peter were understandably overwhelmed but began researching the syndrome in order to assure that they were providing David with the best care and educational treatment. They found a specialized preschool for children with autism, and watched carefully to be sure David was accepted by his peers and teachers.

David's communication and social skills began to improve notably. When he was five years old, David attended a typical kindergarten with a 1:1 aide and continued to progress. Caroline and Peter were excited but still felt they needed to gather as much professional support as possible. They drove two hours to have David evaluated by a nationally renowned group of autism specialists at a university hospital. After meeting with a variety of profession-

als, the consensus was that David did not have autistic disorder after all. They pronounced he had pervasive developmental disorder-not otherwise specified, or "PDD-NOS." Although they were confused about the change in diagnosis, Caroline and Peter investigated this new diagnosis to assure that David was receiving the best treatment approaches.

Today, David is eight years old. Recently, his school's psychologist conducted an annual evaluation and determined that the most appropriate diagnosis for David is Asperger's disorder. At this point, Caroline and Peter feel not only confused but angry. Which diagnosis makes the most sense for their son? Have the treatment and educational strategies they have implemented over the years been appropriate, given the changing diagnostic picture? Does the label assigned to David really matter?

How can one child receive so many diagnoses? Unfortunately, experiences such as this can happen because of periodic confusion within the field regarding differential diagnosis among the autism spectrum disorders. Differential diagnosis involves first determining whether or not an autism spectrum disorder may be present and then pinpointing which ASD diagnosis makes the most sense for a particular child. Having a child with a developmental disorder is difficult enough without adding the burden of multiple diagnoses within the autism spectrum. Most parents have only a general knowledge of "autism" and have never even heard of any of the other autism spectrum disorders. The confusion over which diagnosis is appropriate for your child makes seeking appropriate treatment all the more difficult. If you've been operating under the assumption that your child has one type of ASD and her diagnosis suddenly changes, you may feel your treatment choices no longer fit. This chapter will help parents and professionals understand the characteristics of each autism spectrum disorder so that this type of re-labeling does not occur, except when warranted. In addition, this information will teach you to recognize the differences among the ASDs and between ASDs and other disorders that share similar symptoms and characteristics.

Differential Diagnosis Among the Autism Spectrum Disorders

It is not uncommon for a person to receive more than one diagnosis within the autism spectrum over the course of her lifetime, even though each subcategory is intended to be a distinct diagnosis. When this happens, confusion can occur as parents attempt to understand the system and decide which diagnosis best fits their child. Because each label carries its own prognosis, parents' emotions may fluctuate when their child is reassessed and assigned a new diagnosis. You may find yourself feeling depressed because your child has been "downgraded" from having PDD-NOS to being diagnosed with autistic disorder. At times, it may feel like you're on an emotional roller coaster as you try to keep up with the professionals' differing opinions.

> **Differential diagnosis:** Determining whether or not an ASD may be present and then identifying *which* ASD diagnosis makes the most sense for a particular child.

It is first important to reiterate that there is quite a bit of overlap among the diagnostic criteria for all of the ASDs and therefore confusion is almost inevitable. Also, it is uncommon for a child's symptoms to neatly fit into a given diagnostic category. The table on the next two pages gives guidelines that highlight the most crucial aspects of each of the autism spectrum disorders and will help you better understand where the distinctions lie.

Of the five autism spectrum disorders, the three that overlap the most are autistic disorder, Asperger's disorder, and PDD-NOS. The physical symptoms of Rett's disorder (e.g., head circumference deceleration) plus the presence of excessive hand-wringing make this diagnosis easier to distinguish. Childhood disintegrative disorder is also relatively simple to distinguish because of its later age of onset. However, even this is not always a clear marker. For example, it is not uncommon to hear a parent whose child is diagnosed with autistic disorder describe their

Table 6-1	Differential Diagnosis Among ASDs
Diagnosis	**Essential Features**

Autistic Disorder	A. **Must have _all three_:**
	  1. Qualitative, or measurable, impairments in social skills
	  2. Qualitative impairments in language development
	  3. Restricted and repetitive patterns of behavior, interests, and activities
	B. Usually accompanied by delays in cognitive development and testable IQ<70
	C. Behavioral symptoms observed prior to three years of age

Asperger's Disorder	A. **_Must have both:_**
	  1. Qualitative impairments in social skills
	  2. Restricted and repetitive patterns of behavior, interests, and activities
	B. No delay in language development, although social language may be peculiar
	C. No delay in cognitive development with an IQ at least within average range (i.e., IQ 85 or above)
	D. Symptoms can be rather subtle or even undetected until the child is over three years of age

Pervasive Developmental Disorder-Not Otherwise Specified (PDD-NOS)	A. Must show **_some degree_** of qualitative impairment in:
	  1. Social skills
	    _Or_
	  2. Language skills
	    _Or_ the presence of:
	  3. Restricted and repetitive patterns of behavior or interests

Table 6-1 continued

Diagnosis	Essential Features
Childhood Disintegrative Disorder (CDD)	A. Apparently normal development until at least age two B. Followed by a significant loss of skills in _**at least two**_ of the following areas: 1. Expressive or receptive language 2. Social skills or adaptive behavior 3. Bowel or bladder control 4. Play skills 5. Motor development C. Regression resulting in the presence of _**at least two**_ of the following: 1. Qualitative impairments in social interaction 2. Qualitative impairments in communication 3. Restricted and repetitive patterns of behavior or interests
Rett's Disorder	A. **Must demonstrate _all_ of the following:** 1. Apparently normal early development during infancy 2. Normal head circumference at birth 3. Regression of motor and social skills that occurs between ages five months and two and a half years 4. Deceleration of head circumference growth between the same time period 5. Repetitive hand motions such as hand-wringing or hand-washing actions 6. Poor motor coordination, especially gait and trunk (upper body) movements 7. Although had been able to use hands effectively as an infant, now has difficulty with any tasks that involve hands 8. Severely impaired expressive and receptive language development

child's development as apparently typical until age two and a half or three, followed by a loss of speech and interest in social interactions. This sounds eerily similar to what a parent of a child with childhood disintegrative disorder might describe. Since the age of onset for autistic disorder is "prior to three years of age" and childhood disintegrative disorder calls for typical development until age two, it can sometimes be difficult to distinguish between a child with autistic disorder who demonstrated some loss of skills before age three versus a child with childhood disintegrative disorder.

Questions to Ask Yourself

When attempting to distinguish between the various autism spectrum disorders, it is helpful to answer the following questions. *These are not meant to take the place of a full diagnostic evaluation by a qualified professional, but will arm you with information for the diagnostic process.*

1. *Does your child show all three of the "triad" symptoms (i.e., qualitative impairments in social and language skills coupled with the presence of repetitive and restricted patterns of behavior) or just one or two of these behavioral concerns?* If she displays all three, autistic disorder is the most likely diagnosis, although the other autism spectrum disorders should not be automatically ruled out.

2. *Did your child show typical language development (e.g., spoke single words at one, used short phrases in a communicative fashion by age two) without eventual loss of language skills?* If she demonstrated typical language development and no subsequent loss, autistic disorder is less likely, as most of these children show delays in language acquisition. The appropriate diagnosis is more likely Asperger's disorder or PDD-NOS.

3. *Did your child have a history of typical development across all skill areas (e.g., social, language, motor, self-help skills), followed by a notable regression in skills?* If so, consider childhood disintegrative disorder or Rett's disorder.

4. *Does your child display hand-wringing, limited manual abilities, and a deceleration of head circumference growth?* Rett's disorder is probable.

5. *Does your child show significant cognitive delays (e.g., tests within the mentally retarded range)?* This usually rules out Asperger's disorder, although some people with Asperger's disorder show mild intellectual deficits.

6 . *Does your child have a history of language delay, display only mild qualitative impairments in social and language skills, plus ritualistic or repetitive behaviors, which are relatively minor in intensity and frequency or even have faded?* If so, consider PDD-NOS.

7. *What gender is your child?* Rett's disorder has been reported almost exclusively in females, therefore it is a highly improbable diagnosis if your child is male.

Case Examples

When differentiating the various ASDs, it is important to remember that these disorders involve *clusters* of symptoms. Therefore, it is impossible to distinguish between them contingent upon only one or two characteristics. Below are descriptions of five different people with ASDs. These case studies will hopefully help us *see* the differences among the conditions. As you read each scenario, try to remember the essential features of each of the autism spectrum disorders and predict which diagnosis makes the most sense.

1. / **Bobby:**

Bobby is a four-and-a-half-year-old boy with blond hair and big blue eyes. When greeted by the examiner, Bobby appears unaware of her presence. He makes no eye contact and doesn't turn in her direction when she speaks. Instead, he stares for prolonged periods of time at a videotape playing nearby that his mother describes as one of his favorites. This particular videotape involves songs about the alphabet. As the examiner gathers information from his mother, Bobby watches the videotape and periodically sings along with the person on the tape.

His mother reports that Bobby was the product of a typical pregnancy but that she began to have concerns about him very early on. In contrast to his two older brothers, Bobby was a passive, quiet baby. He stiffened his body when held and would often struggle to be put down. But his early developmental milestones all occurred when expected.

He has never had any particular interest in toys other than to twirl or throw them. He is especially drawn to objects with smooth surfaces and will rub these surfaces in a repetitive manner. Although he can repeat many of the phrases he has heard on his videotapes, he is unable to imitate his parents' verbalizations. He does not yet use speech to communicate. When unable to get across his wishes or needs, Bobby will throw tantrums, frustrating his parents. His tantrums are usually loud and long, involving slamming kitchen cabinets and occasionally hitting his head against the floor. His interactions with his older brothers are characterized by Bobby playing near them but rarely initiating any interactions. However, he will laugh and smile when his oldest brother roughhouses with him.

2. / **Dana:**

Dana is a twenty-three-year-old woman with dark hair and eyes. She is interviewed at the local library, where she works as an assistant, during her break time. When greeted by the examiner, she smiles shyly and says, "Hello." Eye contact is initiated but not sustained. She is able to describe her work responsibilities using clearly articulated, full sentences. She clearly enjoys working in the library and notes that she often stays overtime in order to "catch up on her reading."

Dana's comments reflect a keen mind. At times the wording she chooses is a bit formal and stilted. She describes her childhood as "frequently confusing." Although Dana acquired all of the appropriate skills, such as walking, talking, and self-help skills within the normal range, she has never fully felt comfortable with other people. She reports that she never participated in sports because she tended to be "klutzy." Dana has had no strong romantic relationships and willingly admits this is not a priority for her.

During her free time, Dana enjoys researching animal habitats on the Internet. She can describe any animal's habitat in great detail and proceeds to do so with little awareness of the examiner's waning interest. When she suddenly realizes that her break time is over, Dana abruptly gets up mid-sentence to return to work without even saying "goodbye" to the examiner.

3. / Trevor:

By age two and a half, Trevor was astounding his parents with his extraordinary vocabulary and infectious laugh. He would often bounce onto their bed in the morning with a big hug and smile to start the day. Since he's turned three, however, Trevor has been less affectionate and displays periods of moodiness and social withdrawal. His parents initially attributed the change to a delayed "terrible twos" phase but became more concerned when Trevor started to lose speech. Whereas he had previously been talking in four- or five-word sentences, he was now using only single words to communicate. Trevor also began having toileting accidents, even though he had been fully toilet trained by age two and a half. Trevor's parents took him to the pediatrician, who suggested that they visit a neurologist. The neurological examination showed that Trevor's head circumference was growing at the expected rate; however, he was experiencing some subtle seizure activity.

4. / Matthew:

Matthew is the younger of two sons. His older brother, Tim, is only sixteen months his senior. Mathew's parents often remark that they felt the boys were like twins when they were young. For the most part, Matthew's early development was typical. He was rather independent and tended to play on his own. When others initiated interactions, Mathew usually responded, albeit in a rather limited fashion. His language acquisition was a bit delayed, a fact his parents blamed on his talkative older brother who tended to "speak for Matthew."

As the boys grew a bit older, their parents began to notice more differences between Matthew and Tim. At the preschool the boys attended, Tim was very social and quickly befriended his classmates. However, Matthew preferred playing alongside the other students, without interacting much. Mathew had a relatively large vocabulary but only spoke in abbreviated sentences. Generally, he only spoke when spoken to, rather than spontaneously.

Mathew also began to engage in activities that seemed "quirky" to his parents and teachers. For example, he would hide under a desk if the classroom routine changed. He also insisted on having a laminated list of colors with him at all times, even when sleeping. If Mathew awoke during the night and the list had fallen out of bed, he would cry in desperation until his parents retrieved it. During these moments of distress, he would often rock his body back and forth to calm himself.

5. / Kayla:

As an infant, Kayla was lively and active. She cooed in response to her parents' vocalizations and imitated their simple facial expressions. By the age of three months she was sleeping through the night. Kayla enjoyed playing with her rattle and was able to hold her bottle by the time she was six months old. By her first birthday, Kayla could say approximately twenty words and was able to communicate her basic needs.

Her parents described Kayla as "a real social butterfly." She especially enjoyed going to parties and family get-togethers. However, by the time she turned two, Kayla was less interested in other people. Her parents were also concerned because she began to fall often and even broke her arm during one incident.

During her routine two-year check-up, Kayla's pediatrician noticed that her head circumference was not growing as expected. Concerned, she recommended that Kayla's parents take her for a series of tests at the local university hospital. Two weeks later, on the way to the hospital, her parents noticed that Kayla was wringing her hands over and over again and they wondered if she was anxious about the upcoming tests.

When reading these stories, you may have felt you "recognized" your own child in one of these people. Or, maybe your child displays a combination of the characteristics described in these case studies. As mentioned earlier, most children don't fit neatly into any of the diagnostic categories without some overlap with the other autism spectrum disorders. However, some aspects of the descriptions probably rang true when comparing them to your own experience.

As for differential diagnosis, let's see how successful you were figuring out which of the case studies represented each autism spectrum disorder:

1. In reviewing **Bobby's** developmental history, we should note that his language development was de-

layed, thus making Asperger's disorder, childhood disintegrative disorder, or Rett's disorder unlikely. So, we are left with autistic disorder or PDD-NOS. Considering that Bobby strongly demonstrates all three of the "triad" of symptoms (impairment in communication, social skills, and ritualistic behavior), a diagnosis of **autistic disorder** is the most logical choice.

2. **Dana's** symptoms, on the other hand, are relatively less severe than Bobby's. Dana is verbal, appears quite bright, and holds competitive employment. At the same time, she is clearly preoccupied with her own interests and has difficulty interpreting and responding to social interactions. We should also note that her language development was normal even though her motor coordination was somewhat delayed. Overall, her symptoms best match **Asperger's disorder**.

3. **Trevor's** early development was within the average range if not rather advanced. He was motivated to interact with others and acquired language easily. These early signs discourage a diagnosis of autistic disorder or PDD-NOS. Trevor's regression in skills leads us to consider either childhood disintegrative disorder or Rett's disorder. Considering the lack of physiological symptoms (e.g., head circumference growth plateau) or hand-wringing, plus the fact that Trevor is male, it is likely that **childhood disintegrative disorder** is the most appropriate diagnosis.

4. Early on, **Matthew's** development did not cause any concern for his parents. He was a bit of a "loner" but responded to others' interactions to some extent. He developed speech somewhat later than usual, which tends to rule out Asperger's disorder. He has some unusual behaviors, especially his reactions to transi-

tions and his special interest in colors. He also demonstrates repetitive rocking. However, he generally functions well in his world. For example, he is attending a typical preschool with relative success. Overall, Matthew's symptoms most closely match a diagnosis of **PDD-NOS**.

5. **Kayla's** development is striking in that her early developmental milestones all occurred when expected. She seemed interested in social interactions and her language development was typical as well. However, Kayla's parents recognized when she was two that her skills were regressing. Perhaps the two most pronounced symptoms were the decelerated head growth coupled with the demonstration of hand-wringing, both of which point clearly to a diagnosis of **Rett's disorder**.

Hopefully the above examples will help you better understand the kinds of questions an experienced professional may ask herself when making a diagnosis.

Why is Pinpointing the Right Diagnosis So Important?

Clearly, differentiating among the five autism spectrum disorders is by no means an easy task. So, why do it? There are a number of reasons why attempts at differential diagnosis are worthwhile:

- **Treatment:** Treatment strategies that are implemented should always be linked specifically to a diagnosis. Techniques that make the most sense for a child with severe autistic disorder would not be appropriate for a child with Asperger's disorder. (Specific techniques will be reviewed in Chapter Nine.) Similarly, a child with Rett's disorder may require medical intervention due to the heightened possibility of seizures.

- **Educational Placement:** Many educational systems rely heavily on a child's diagnosis when determining appropriate classroom placement. Children with different types of ASDs often require distinct classroom placements, opportunities for mainstreaming or inclusion, and support services within the school system.

- **Research:** Right now a great deal of research on autism is happening with the goal of determining causal factors, effective teaching treatments, and medications. Examining each type of ASD separately may help in pinpointing specific causes underlying each disorder as well as the most effective treatments across ASDs.

- **Impact on Eventual Progress:** Research has repeatedly shown that early diagnosis can make a significant difference in terms of a child's eventual prognosis. It appears that the brain of a child under age six is often able to be flexible in its development; that is, areas of the brain that work well are able to take over functions that the less efficient areas of the brain cannot perform well. This idea will be explained further in Chapter Nine when describing the importance of early intervention.

  It is important to emphasize that misdiagnosis may impact a child's overall prognosis if it leads to the loss of opportunities for appropriate early intervention services. This can also result from a professional using a "milder" label such as "language delayed" or even PDD-NOS to lessen the impact on the parents when, in fact, a diagnosis of autistic disorder is actually warranted. By giving an inappropriate diagnosis, the professional may be inadvertently hindering the child's ability to receive early, appropriate treatment.

Differential Diagnosis Between ASDs and Other, Similar Conditions

There are certain developmental disorders that have similar characteristics to autism spectrum disorders and can create confusion during the diagnostic process. It is important for parents to be aware of these conditions so they can be absolutely certain their child's diagnosis is accurate. At the same time, it is recommended that parents not spend an undue amount of time mulling over the possibility of one of these other conditions if the diagnostic signs all point towards an ASD. These include:

Fragile X Syndrome:

Fragile X syndrome is the single most common inherited cause of mental retardation. This condition, which can affect both genders, is far more common in males and can be identified through DNA testing. Linked to an abnormality of the X chromosome, this condition is characterized by distinct facial features, including a long face, large and low-set ears, a prominent chin, and larger than normal testicles. Research shows that up to one third of males with fragile X syndrome also meet the diagnostic criteria for PDD-NOS and a smaller group meet the criteria for autistic disorder. However, only three to five percent of boys with autism have fragile X syndrome. Although this is a small percentage, it is recommended that chromosomal testing be conducted for all children with autism in order to determine whether fragile X syndrome is present. Chromosomal testing can be done easily via a blood test.

Scientific research has shown that fragile X syndrome is caused by genetic abnormalities that are passed down by the mother. Therefore, having this knowledge will help with family planning (there is a fifty percent chance that any future pregnancies will result in another child with fragile X syndrome). Also, results from chromosomal testing may provide parents with a better understanding of the cause(s) underlying their child's ASD.

Although there is no "cure" for fragile X syndrome, the mere knowledge of the cause(s) is often helpful for parents' emotional acceptance of a developmental disorder. People with fragile X syndrome are often awkward and shy socially, as compared to people with autism who tend to be aloof. People with fragile X syndrome may display various self-stimulatory behaviors, over-sensitivity to sound or touch, abnormalities of speech, and limited eye contact and attention span. Developmental delays across many skill areas such as language, motor skills, self-help skills, and the like are common.

Landau-Kleffner Syndrome (LKS):

Landau-Kleffner syndrome (also known as LKS and Acquired Childhood Epileptic Aphasia) is a very rare condition that shares many similar behavioral symptoms with ASDs. LKS is most often confused with childhood disintegrative disorder rather than one of the other ASDs, since both CDD and LKS are characterized by normal early development followed by a regression in skills.

Children with LKS tend to have periods of staring, odd oral movements, hyperactivity, and difficulty processing and responding to language. Similar to kids with ASDs, children with LKS may have limited eye contact, repetitive behaviors, and an insistence on sameness (aversion to change). The most definitive way to distinguish between these two conditions is with an EEG (measures brain activity), which almost always reflects abnormal central nervous system activity if the child actually has Landau-Kleffner syndrome. Fortunately, if LKS is identified via an EEG, antiseizure medications can often be very helpful and up to eighty percent of the children show significant progress.

Mental Retardation (MR):

Approximately seventy percent of people with autistic disorder function within the mentally retarded range. Of course, it is possible to have mental retardation without the presence of an ASD. When considering individuals with mental retardation only, IQs usually fall within the mild to moderate levels of mental retardation. People with severe or profound mental retardation generally show significant impairments in language and social skills. Individuals with severe or profound mental retardation may demonstrate repetitive and seemingly nonfunctional behaviors such as rocking or repeatedly tapping an object.

However, in contrast to ASDs, severe mental retardation alone involves an overall pervasive developmental delay rather than a pervasive *disordered* developmental delay. For example, a ten-year-old with severe mental retardation *without an ASD* may have the skills of a two-year-old across *all skill areas* (i.e., language, self-help, motor, social skills, etc.). In contrast, autism spectrum disorders involve a pattern of peaks and valleys across skill areas such as seen in a twelve-year-old child with age appropriate self-help skills but no speech.

Schizophrenia:

In the early years, ASDs and schizophrenia were inadvertently linked, resulting in much confusion and poor treatment decisions. Kanner's use of the word "autistic," which had previously been used to describe individuals with schizophrenia, caused some people to assume that these two conditions were similar. Although individuals with schizophrenia and ASDs both have difficulty relating to others and may show unusual speech, there are many ways these two conditions are different. The features of schizophrenia do not usually emerge until a child is much older than three years old, the cut-off age for the onset of symptoms of an ASD. In fact, schizophrenia does not usually emerge until a child becomes an adolescent or even young adult. Prior to the onset of schizophrenic symptoms, nothing appears unusual about a child's development. Also, the hallmark of schizophrenia is the presence of hallucinations or delusions, which are not present in autism spectrum disorders.

Speech and Language Disorders:

Children with speech and language disorders usually show delays in speech acquisition or difficulties in articulation. Sometimes professionals consider the presence of an ASD when, in fact, a child has a severe speech and language disorder. Often this confusion takes place when a child is four years old or younger, before she has had the opportunity to receive effective and intensive speech therapy. It is not uncommon for a young child with a severe speech and language disorder to avoid social interactions, since most of these involve speech and are particularly intimidating and difficult for them. This tendency can masquerade as a symptom of autism.

It is unlikely, however, that you will see the other signs of an ASD, such as restrictive and repetitive behaviors or interests. Furthermore, children with speech and language disorders tend to demonstrate communicative intent; that is, even though they have limited ability to express their needs or wants through speech, they often put great effort into developing nonverbal means of communicating, such as signing, pointing, gesturing, etc. In contrast, children with ASDs don't appear to be motivated to communicate with others. As a child with a severe speech and language disorder gains improved speech or she is provided an augmentative means of communicating, such as a language board or voice-synthesized communication device, social skills tend to improve notably.

Aphasia:

Another speech and language disorder that is sometimes mistaken for an ASD is aphasia. Aphasia is a condition in which a person is unable to produce or comprehend speech, due to some type of injury to the brain. These individuals may be unable to put their thoughts into words or may say sentences that do not seem to make sense. They may also have difficulty following instructions. Incidences of aphasia occur most commonly in individuals who have suffered a stroke, but may also be the result of brain trauma, tumors, or infections. A person with aphasia may have difficulty speaking, understanding speech, or reading. In contrast to people with ASDs, people with aphasia almost invariably have a typical developmental history. They are interested in communicating but have difficulty putting thoughts into words. They do not demonstrate the ritualistic and repetitive behaviors that are a hallmark of an autism spectrum disorder.

Nonverbal Learning Disorders (NLD):

Nonverbal learning disorders is a category of disorders that has been recently identified. In contrast to individuals with ASDs, people with NLD show strengths in the area of speech development. They are usually of average, if not above average intelligence. They generally demonstrate clear strengths in the areas of reading and spelling. There are certain shared symptoms among NLD and ASDs, including difficulties with transitions, deficits in social awareness, and over-sensitivity to sensory input. However, unlike people with ASDs, people with NLD do not display ritualistic and repetitive behaviors or qualitative impairments in communication. The ASD that is most often mistaken for a nonverbal learning disorder is Asperger's disorder, since both conditions involve average to above average intelligence as compared to other ASDs, which are more likely to involve cognitive impairments.

Sensory Impairments:

Children born deaf or blind often demonstrate behaviors that mimic some of the symptoms of ASD. For example, young children who cannot hear may be less responsive to interpersonal interactions until they have developed a means of communication, such as signing or reading lips. Similarly, interest in interpersonal interactions will increase if the child has gained improved hearing via hearing aids, a cochlear implant, or the like. Blind children may demonstrate self-stimulatory behaviors such as tapping their eyes in a repetitive fashion or rocking. These self-stimulatory behaviors may serve to help alleviate boredom stemming from the decreased sensory input inherent to being blind. However, as these children grow older and learn compensatory skills to override their sensory impairments, their social and communication skills tend to improve significantly and the incidence of self-stimulatory behaviors decreases as well. This is not to say that children who are deaf or blind cannot also have an ASD. However, the incidence of ASDs in children with sensory impairments is no more common than is seen in the general population.

Reactive Attachment Disorder (RAD):

The primary characteristic of children with reactive attachment disorder is an inability to relate to other people prior to five years of age. These children, like those with ASD, may fail to initiate or respond to social interactions, or show an inability to discriminate relationships appropriately and act accordingly (e.g., being overly friendly to strangers). In contrast to ASDs, which are clearly physiological in origin, RAD is caused by a history of the child being abused in some manner or having had no consistent caregiver and therefore no opportunity to develop strong attachments. Although some of these children continue to demonstrate developmental and interpersonal concerns throughout their childhood and sometimes into their adult lives, others show a marked decrease in symptoms, and an ability to build strong relationships with others once they are provided a nurturing and supportive home-life.

Obsessive-Compulsive Disorder (OCD):

Individuals with obsessive-compulsive disorder experience recurrent obsessions that cause anxiety (e.g., worrying that they will be exposed to germs). These obsessions lead them to engage in repetitive behaviors or rituals, called compulsions, that are meant to alleviate the anxiety brought on by the obsessions (e.g., washing their hands repeatedly to kill germs). These ritualistic behaviors can look a lot like those of people with ASD. People with autism spectrum disorders do not realize that their repetitive actions are nonfunctional or problematic. In contrast to individuals with ASDs, people with OCD recognize that their repetitive behaviors are irrational but feel compelled to continue them in order to calm their anxiety. The fact that people with OCD do not have the same problems with communication and social skills as those with ASD is another distinction between these groups.

Social Phobia:

People with social phobia have an excessive fear of situations that require interpersonal interactions, especially with unfamiliar people. They actively avoid social situations, which cause them high levels of anxiety. As children, they may, for example, act out their anxiety through tantrums and crying jags when in public. Although some people with ASDs appear anxious when in public, this anxiety may be better explained by their difficulty processing information in highly stimulating environments. One little girl with autistic disorder exclaimed to fellow shoppers while at the mall, "Slow down! I'm getting dizzy!" In contrast to children with ASDs, children with social phobia are better able to form friendships. In addition, people with social phobia do not display unusual communication or repetitive and ritualistic behaviors as do people with autism spectrum disorders.

Dual Diagnosis: When ASDs Overlap with Other Conditions

A number of children with autism spectrum disorders also meet the diagnostic criteria for other developmental disabilities or mental health disorders. For example, as described below, in addition to the possibility of having an ASD coupled with mental retardation, ASDs can also coexist with mental health disorders, such as a mood or anxiety disorder.

Why is this important to know? When a child has more than one condition, otherwise known as a dual diagnosis or "comorbidity," each diagnosis should be considered when developing treatment plans, deciding on medications, and making other decisions based on need. Sometimes professionals are hesitant to give a child more than one diagnosis, or label. Although a child may meet the diagnostic criteria for both an ASD as well as a previously diagnosed condition, many professionals refrain from adding the new diagnosis for a variety of reasons. Maybe they want to spare the family from feeling overwhelmed by another diagnosis. Or, the professional may fall into a trap known as "diagnostic overshadowing," which is the assumption that the previous diagnosis overrides any new ones and may in fact explain the presence of the problem behaviors. For example, a small group of children with Down syndrome also have an autism spectrum disorder. This dual diagnosis is known as DS/ASD. In a case such as this, a professional may attribute the child's autistic characteristics (e.g., communication deficits or self-stimulatory behaviors) to the presence of Down syndrome, rather than acknowledging an ASD may be present as well.

When determining if a child with an already known condition may also have an ASD, a professional should look for the same "triad" of symptoms reviewed earlier, i.e., the presence of qualitative impairments in social skills, qualitative impairments in communication, and the presence of repetitive or ritualistic behaviors. Remember, there must be a *clustering* of all three of these characteristics in order to consider the presence of autism. That is, the presence of only one or two of these developmental differences is *not* sufficient to warrant the additional diagnosis of an ASD. For example, while an individual with obsessive-compulsive disorder (OCD) may show repetitive and ritualistic behaviors, she rarely displays the atypical communication and social development seen with an ASD.

ASDs and Mental Retardation

More often than not, when a child with an ASD has a dual diagnosis, the other condition is mental retardation. As mentioned, upwards of seventy percent of people with ASDs have mental retardation. Most of these children with both an ASD and mental retardation test within the mild range of mental retardation (i.e., IQ between fifty and seventy), but it is possible for a child with moderate or severe mental retardation to have an autism spectrum disorder as well.

What does a child with an autism spectrum disorder *and* mental retardation "look like"? Remember, a child with mental retardation has pervasive delays across *all* developmental areas, whereas a child with only ASD has inconsistent delays. A child with both mental retardation and an autism spectrum disorder will exhibit developmental delays across all areas, but also show *qualitative impairments (i.e., peaks and valleys)* in these areas. For example, she may have a relatively strong vocabulary but not be able to maintain a conversation using this vocabulary. Or, she may show minimal interest in playing with others even though she is more than capable of initiating an interaction when there is an immediate need (e.g., thirst, hunger). Both of these descriptions are examples of "qualitative impairments" (peaks and valleys) within the areas of social and language skills that might be seen in a child with both mental retardation and an ASD.

It is also important to remember that in order to receive a dual diagnosis of ASD plus mental retardation, a child must also demonstrate repetitive and ritualistic behaviors as well as qualitative impairments in the areas of social and language skills. For example, one child with both mental retardation and autistic disorder displayed repetitive hand and head movements, insisted that her toys be lined up in a predetermined fashion, and wanted to talk about trains all day. Chapter Seven will provide additional information regarding the coexistence of an ASD with mental retardation and related issues.

ASDs and Mental Health Disorders

Every so often, a child will have a mental health disorder as well as an autism spectrum disorder. For example, some children with autism spectrum disorders can show the characteristics of a mood disorder, such as depression. In contrast to most people with depression alone, the majority of people with ASDs, especially children, have great difficulty identifying and expressing their feelings of sadness. Instead, their symptoms may include loss of interest in previously preferred activities, changes in sleeping or eating patterns, periods of unexplained tearfulness, or an increase in irritability or challenging behaviors.

Another type of mental health disorder that can be associated with ASD is an anxiety disorder. Of the anxiety disorders that exist, the one most likely to co-occur with an ASD is "Generalized Anxiety Disorder." This condition involves the individual feeling worried and anxious the majority of the time with no clear reason. Other behavioral signs include irritability, muscle tension, fatigue, restlessness, and disturbed sleep.

It is more common for the parent of a child already diagnosed with an ASD to wonder if she also has a mental health condition, as opposed to the other way around. This is because most mental health conditions do not become evident until a child is at least school aged. In contrast, the signs of an autism spectrum disorder are evident at a much younger age. Therefore, the diagnosis of an autism spectrum disorder usually precedes that of a mental health condition.

Due to the fact that children with ASDs have limited communication skills, especially in the area of expressing feelings, it is often difficult to determine whether or not they also have a mental health disorder. More often than not, the professional needs to rely upon the existence of overt behavior (e.g., loss of appetite, refusing to participate in previously preferred activities) and parental report rather than expecting the child to express her feelings. Nonetheless, an experienced clinician will be able to discern whether or not a mental health disorder is also present.

It is often difficult for parents to find professionals who are willing to recognize that a child's overall profile may reflect more than one diagnosis. However, if you suspect that your child with ASD may also have a developmental disability or mental health disorder, it is essential to keep searching until you find a professional who can look at your child's unique set of skills and needs in a comprehensive manner. Likewise, if you believe your child has an ASD in addition to an existing developmental disability or mental health disorder, seek out a professional who will explore this possibility with you. Only by having a full understanding of your child's overall situation can the most effective and successful treatment plan be developed. Certain treatments and medications may be more appropriate for a child with a dual diagnosis, so viewing the entire picture may open the door for a more expansive intervention package. Not doing so could result in a dampening of your child's overall progress and ability to cope with life's pressures.

Parents Speak

The period prior to diagnosis was very challenging and frustrating and, at times, we felt helpless.

Fortunately, Patrick is not diagnosed with anything other than mild autism. However, I still prefer the term PDD. Some say it is too vague, but I think it symbolizes a milder form of the condition, which applies best to Patrick. When he was three, I would have probably slapped anyone who called him autistic. Now, the label is much less important to me, as long as the person using it is helping my son.

7 | The Diagnostic Process

The Roberts Family

Bill and Tiffany Roberts always knew something was different about their young daughter, Christine. From an early age, she did not enjoy being cuddled and rarely made eye contact. Christine was disinterested in people and spent many hours lining up plastic letters in a ritualistic fashion. She was a moody child, often having tantrums and screaming loudly for no apparent reason. She never slept through the night and her parents were exhausted.

When Christine was two, the Roberts expressed their concerns to their pediatrician, who in turn referred them to a local team of specialists in childhood disorders. The night before the appointment with the diagnostic team, Tiffany and Bill were so anxious they could hardly sleep. How long would the evaluation take? What would it entail? Would Christine become agitated and pitch a fit? What should they do if this happened? What diagnosis would be determined? While it would be a relief to finally find out what was going on, perhaps they were rushing things and should just wait and see if Christine's development improved....

For parents, gathering information and participating in evaluations to determine the cause(s) of their child's developmental differences can be particularly stressful. While you may clearly recognize the need to address your child's atypical development, it is not unusual to want to deny the problem and put off evaluation, favoring a "wait and see" approach. This can be a very difficult time and parents often find themselves unprepared for what comes next.

If you are like most parents, you have been concerned that something is "wrong" for some time, but now comes the day when knowledgeable experts are hopefully going to give you some insight and guidance. To be an active, participating member of your child's diagnostic evaluation rather than an anxiety-ridden observer, it is important that you prepare yourself ahead of time for what to expect. Although it's natural to want to drag your heels at this stage, keep in mind you are doing your child a tremendous favor by getting the earliest diagnosis possible. This chapter will provide the necessary knowledge and tools to guide you through the diagnostic maze and give you the confidence you need to fully participate in the process.

What Else Could it Be?

There are certain medical or environmental conditions that should always be ruled out when determining whether or not a child has an autism spectrum disorder. Your child's hearing should always be assessed in order to rule out whether his lack of response to verbal input is due to a hearing impairment. It is wise to take your child to an audiologist for an evaluation before scheduling an ASD evaluation. If your child is unable to respond to a traditional hearing test because he has difficulty following basic directions, there are other options available. Special assessment procedures can monitor neurological responses in a child's central nervous system, establishing whether or not he is hearing various sound frequencies. It is also important to rule out any history of maltreatment when the child was younger, as neglected or abused children can at times become very socially withdrawn and non-communicative. This is especially relevant if your child was adopted. For other conditions that need to be ruled out, please refer to the section entitled *Differential Diagnosis Between ASDs and Other, Similar Conditions* in Chapter Six.

How Do I Set Up an Evaluation?

There are various avenues you can take to set up an evaluation for your child. Many parents rely upon their pediatrician's advice and support when looking at possible settings for the assessment to take place. Although many pediatricians are helpful in this regard, others have little knowledge of the process involved in obtaining a diagnostic assessment for an ASD. Therefore parents may need to find guidance through other avenues, such as a state agency. Each state government system includes an agency that provides support and funding for services to children with developmental differences. Refer to the Resource Guide in the back of the book for detailed information. Often, case managers, service coordinators, intake personnel, and social workers are assigned to a family through state agencies, or your child's school or Early Intervention services and can advise you what support services are available in your community.

Unfortunately, parents frequently wind up setting up the evaluation completely on their own with little support from professionals. They may find themselves calling various hospitals, professional assessment settings and the like in their quest to find a setting that has a knowledgeable and experienced diagnostic team. Needless to say, this can be a tiring and confusing endeavor. However, recognize that the time spent setting up the assessment will pay off in the long run if the end result is a better understanding of your child's needs and diagnosis.

Once parents have decided upon the best setting for their child's evaluation, commonly they are put on a waiting list that requires they wait months before the actual evaluation. If this happens to you, the old adage "the squeaky wheel gets the grease" applies. Let the scheduling secretary know that you are willing to come in on short notice if a cancellation occurs and call in frequently to inquire about cancellations. Also, it can be helpful if your pediatrician or other professional involved with your child calls to request that the assessment date be sooner. If the agency has mailed a questionnaire for you to fill out, make sure to complete and return the form as soon as possible so that this is not a cause for delay.

Who Should Be Involved?

Ideally, a multidisciplinary team should be involved when conducting a comprehensive evaluation of your child. A multidisciplinary team, sometimes referred to as an interdisciplinary or transdisciplinary team, is a group of professionals from a variety of fields. Each brings his own areas of expertise to the evaluation process. Professionals that should almost certainly be involved are a psychologist, psychiatrist, speech and language pathologist (SLP), and a neurologist. It may also be advantageous to include a physical therapist (PT) if there are concerns about your child's gross motor development, or an occupational therapist (OT) if your child shows difficulties with fine motor activities or sensory input. While gross motor activities involve large movements such as walking or running, fine motor skills usually entail more discrete movements such as pointing or picking up small objects. As mentioned in Chapter Five, some children with ASDs demonstrate unusual reactions to sensory input such as becoming upset when touched or when a mechanical noise is heard. At times an Occupational Therapist can both assess these sensory concerns as well as provide strategies that can be helpful in alleviating them.

An ideal multidisciplinary team should include a:
- Psychologist
- Psychiatrist
- Speech and Language Pathologist (SLP)
- Neurologist
- Physical Therapist (PT)
- Occupational Therapist (OT)

How do parents determine whether or not a given evaluation team is competent to evaluate their child? It is imperative that the members of the multidisciplinary team all have extensive experience with ASDs. It is within your rights to ask one of the team ahead of time about the members' backgrounds and professional experience in order to assess whether or not they have sufficient expertise in this area. Ask questions such as: What training have the professionals had related to autism spectrum disorders? How many children have they diagnosed who were suspected of having an autism spectrum disorder? Are all the team members equally qualified? Can they provide any written material that outlines their background? If the team does not have sufficient experience, ask one of the team members to refer you to a setting with the required expertise and background. Or, as will be discussed later in this chapter, parents can create their own diagnostic team by identifying individual professionals in the field, each of whom are qualified, and ask that they work together to evaluate their child.

Although it is convenient for the multidisciplinary team to meet your child as a group, sometimes this is not practical and the parents may need to take their child to be evaluated by each professional separately. For example, if your child cannot tolerate a prolonged evaluation with many professionals, it may make more sense to conduct each evaluation separately. The specific order your child visits with professionals is unimportant. Regardless of how the evaluations are scheduled, there should be ongoing communication between the professionals involved so that the diagnostic evaluation report is a well-rounded overview of your child's developmental profile.

Each professional should document his findings to assure complete understanding by everyone involved. It is wise to state this expectation clearly ahead of time to the team and also request a copy of the final evaluation. Ideally, the final report should incorporate the findings of all the evaluators plus a summary with recommendations. It is important that you schedule a time to sit down with the team to discuss the report afterwards. This will afford you the opportunity to ask any and all questions regarding the results. It may also be helpful to discuss the results with a particular team member if you have specific questions within their area of expertise.

Where Should a Diagnostic Evaluation Take Place?

Diagnostic evaluations for autism spectrum disorders can take place in a variety of settings. There are clinics and university-based settings across the country that specialize in autism spectrum disorders. Unfortunately, there may not be one within your local area. (Often, if determining this is the best option, families will travel the day before an evaluation and stay overnight in a hotel so they can be fresh for the meeting.) University hospitals tend to be one of the best locations to schedule a comprehensive evaluation because so many professionals are available under the same roof. University-based clinics or hospitals also tend to be more on the cutting edge of recent research and diagnostic measures. If it is feasible for you to take your child to this type of setting, even if it involves a bit more traveling, it is highly recommended. Local chapters of the Autism Society of America (ASA) can be helpful in identifying which university-based settings are best qualified in your area. See the Resource Guide at the back of this book for information about how to contact the ASA and other organizations.

You can also set up a diagnostic evaluation for your child at a group medical practice, preferably one that supports the multidisciplinary team approach outlined above. You can ask your pediatrician or another professional involved with your child's care about medical groups in the area. If neither of these two options are available to you, it may be necessary to create your own multidisciplinary team by identifying various experts in the field from different disciplines and then taking your child to see each one individually. Again, network with involved professionals and other parents to identify a psychologist, neurologist, speech therapist, and other relevant specialists and then set up appointments with each. Although this can be difficult and time-consuming, it is essential to receive the best assessment possible. It is to your advantage to insist that each of the professionals involved communicate with each other so that you have a unified support team when making diagnostic and treatment decisions. You can facilitate this communication process by providing a list of names, phone numbers, and email addresses to each member. It is often advantageous to request that one of the professionals be the "team leader" who will help to coordinate the process, or your pediatrician can serve in this role.

It is also possible to have your child evaluated by your local state agency or school system. These agencies may be divided according to the age of the child, e.g., "Early Intervention" for children under five, and "School-Age" programs for children aged five and older. The advantage of this route is that the evaluation will be at no cost to you and the professionals involved may have knowledge about local services available, such as specialized classrooms or local agencies that set up in-home treatment programs. However, you need to investigate whether or not the local school system or state agency has a strong background in autism spectrum disorders so that you can be secure in their findings. School evaluations will be discussed in more detail later in this chapter.

How Can I Prepare Ahead of Time?

Never lose track of the fact that you are an essential member of the diagnostic team. You know your child better than anyone else, and therefore your input is crucial. Do not fear that the "experts" will discount your comments because you are "just a parent." Since autism spectrum disorders are diagnosed purely from a behavioral standpoint (i.e., determining whether or not certain behaviors are present), the professionals need to know what *you* have observed from the moment your child was born. They only have a brief opportunity to observe and gather information

> Never lose track of the fact that you are an essential member of the diagnostic team. You know your child better than anyone else, and therefore your input is crucial.

about your child, as compared to your years of experience. Both parents should make every effort to attend the evaluation in order to impart as much knowledge as possible to the professionals. If a grandparent or teacher is especially involved with your child, it may prove worthwhile to have him attend the evaluation as well.

Preparing the Evaluators

In order to participate in the diagnostic process in the most effective manner, you need to do some up-front preparation. Send information about your child to the diagnostic team ahead of time in order to help them be ready for your meeting. Often, agencies have their own standardized form that parents need to fill out prior to their first consultation. This form usually includes questions regarding your child's development as well your current concerns. Fill out the form and return it as soon as possible in order to assure that the diagnostic team has sufficient time to read your answers before the day of the evaluation. If the agency does not provide a form, it is useful to write up relevant information regarding your child's development and send it to the team ahead of time for their perusal.

Help Prepare the Diagnostic Team

Consider sending the following information about your child to the diagnostic team *before* your scheduled evaluation:

- Pregnancy/delivery information;
- When developmental milestones occurred such as sitting independently, walking, talking, toileting, etc.;
- Relevant medical history and concerns (e.g., operations, illnesses, seizures);
- History of any medications that have been prescribed;
- Alternative treatments you've used;
- Any early intervention services that were provided;
- Educational history to date;

The team will benefit from receiving many types of information about your child prior to the meeting. Make copies of all evaluations that have been conducted to date (e.g., speech assessments, screening tests conducted by early intervention teams, etc.) and send them to the diagnostic team for their perusal. (Also bring copies of the evaluations with you to the diagnostic evaluation in case you need to refer to them.) If possible, you may want to send along an edited videotape that shows snippets of your child's development through the years.

Before the meeting, make a detailed and comprehensive list of your concerns, including specific descriptions of your child's atypical behaviors or developmental trends. For example, if your child stares at fans, exhibits aggression, or is unable to feed himself, include these behaviors on your list. Make note of the duration of each behavioral concern (i.e., how long it has been happening), as well as the frequency (i.e., how often you see it). Include any life history factors that you feel may have an impact on your child's behavior or development, such as a death in the family, or a recent move, etc. Make note of any medical concerns or conditions your child has ever experienced. Include results of hearing and vision tests. Write down if your child has had chronic ear infections or tubes inserted as this may have affected speech

- List of behavioral concerns you believe should be addressed;
- History of any developmental differences or mental health disorders in the family (e.g., maternal grandmother has bipolar disorder);
- Results of any previous testing, including hearing and vision exams;
- Quotes from report cards and other teacher evaluations;
- Areas where your child has done relatively well (e.g., maybe your child is especially adept at motor activities such as dancing); and
- Videotape of your child (optional).

acquisition. List any developmental differences or mental health disorders on either side of the family, as these may be helpful in making a differential diagnosis. Of course, add any other information you feel may be pertinent.

It is also helpful to the evaluators to know all the treatment strategies you have implemented with your child and their relative effectiveness. Bring a list of strategies and programs you've used, including ones that address skill deficits (e.g., how you have attempted to promote speech), and behavioral challenges (e.g., what techniques you have implemented to alleviate aggression). Having this knowledge ahead of time will give the evaluators a better understanding of what works, and does not work, with your own child.

Writing down all of this information ahead of time will assure that you cover all of the issues while at the diagnostic evaluation rather than lamenting afterwards that you forgot to mention some crucial factors. In fact, organizing all of this information into a loose-leaf binder or file folder that you can continually add to is an excellent idea. At the beginning of the notebook, keep a running list of the names and phone numbers of each professional who has been involved with your child. This will become an invaluable resource for years to come.

Readying Your Child

Keep in mind that the diagnostic assessment may pose various challenges for you and your child. Understandably, many young children with and without developmental differences find unfamiliar settings and unfamiliar people unnerving. Your child may get upset by changes in his daily routine and therefore will be troubled to find himself at the assessment during a time usually reserved for another activity. Also, if the assessment includes more rigorous testing, your child will likely find the evaluation a distressing experience.

There are various ways to prepare your child for the assessment, depending on his strengths and weaknesses. For example, if your child understands much of what is said to him, you may be able to merely explain that you are going to a new place filled with new people. It is beneficial *not* to use the term "doctor," as children often associate this word with needles and other uncomfortable memories. Rather, refer to the individuals involved as people who would like to get to know your child. If possible, give your child a timeframe as to how long you will be at this new place and agree on a preferred activity that will take place immediately after the assessment (e.g., going to the video store). Providing a reinforcing item or activity will help your child look forward to this new experience rather than dwell on the unknown.

Some children benefit from acting-out, or role-playing, an upcoming assessment. For example, a pretend clinic can be created in your family room, which includes a waiting room, receptionist's desk, testing rooms, etc. Explain and then model expected behaviors as if you were at the evaluation. If you have personally visited the clinic already, try to make the pretend clinic as much like the actual setting as possible. Talk out loud as you model going through the assessment (e.g., "Now we're going to see Miss Carol. She'll ask us to say lots of sounds.") Now switch roles and prompt your child to demonstrate the appropriate behaviors you have just modeled. Praise your child for participating in the role-play activity and repeat the process at least a few times prior to the evaluation.

More often, children scheduled for a diagnostic assessment for an ASD have minimal ability to understand the explanations and role-playing described above. In these cases, more creative methods of readying your child can be considered. For example, if the evaluation setting is relatively close by, you could visit the location and give your child the opportunity to become familiar with the layout of the building. Point out items of interest that you think your child will enjoy (e.g., toys in the waiting room, a ceiling fan). Make sure to communicate your intention to visit the setting ahead of time so that receptionists and other staff are not taken off guard by your presence. Also, staff may be willing to give you a brief guided tour of the facility. Bring a camera along and take pictures of various rooms and people so you can later use these to further prepare your child for what is to come. Another way to ready your child for this new experience is to use Social Stories. As we'll discuss in more detail in Chapter Nine, this involves creating an individualized storybook with pictures and written content related to a situation or event. For instance, you might write a storybook about "Visiting the Clinic," which includes the photographs you took when you visited, as well as brief text about what your child might experience during the evaluation process. It makes sense to write the story from the perspective of your child. For example, one page may read, "When I first get to the clinic, I can play with the toy fire engine," coupled with a picture of your child playing with this toy. For more information regarding Social Stories, please refer to the numerous resources developed by Carol Gray (e.g., Gray & Leigh, 2002).

Bringing along your child's favorite toys or objects will help him feel more secure while at the assessment. Preferred foods or drinks should also be easily accessible throughout the evaluation and provided periodically as a means to help your child feel comfortable and happy. Other strategies to help the process are reviewed below.

What Will the Evaluation Process 'Look Like'?

Each diagnostic team has its own way of conducting a diagnostic evaluation. Therefore, it is impossible to know ahead of time exactly what you will experience, personally. However, there are some common practices among evaluation teams. The professionals will usually start by interviewing you about your child's developmental history. They may ask you detailed questions about each and every step of your child's development, so be prepared to provide this type of information using the notes you have prepared. It is helpful to bring along a "baby book" if it includes notations regarding your child's early development, such as when he first sat, walked, spoke, etc. The entire team may jointly conduct the interview, or you may meet with each team member individually. Hopefully, you will not have to answer the same questions over and over again if separate meetings are scheduled, but this is not uncommon.

If the entire diagnostic team is on-site during the evaluation, professionals may take turns interacting with your child while other team members interview you. Interactions between your child and each team member should seem low-key and natural. Many assessments involve evaluating your child's abilities by engaging him with games or toys so that he is unaware he's being evaluated. Team members will nonchalantly attempt to engage your child in conversations in order to assess communication skills. They will also be constantly observing your child's behaviors and reactions to gain a better understanding of his development and what might be an appropriate diagnosis. Some clinics have two-way mirrors that allow parents to watch their child being assessed, which can be reassuring for parents who are uncomfortable with the idea of being separated from their child.

One of the team members may attempt to take your child to another room while you remain with another team member. If your child becomes excessively upset or you personally don't feel comfortable being separated from your child, directly express your preference to have your child remain with you. Discuss this possibility with the team ahead of time in order to find out how they will respond to this issue. It may also be advantageous for you to stay with your child until he has warmed up to the environment and the evaluators and then attempt to leave him again. Sometimes the team can gain important information by observing your child without you being there (e.g., does the child recognize their parent's absence? How does the child respond when reunited with his parents?)

It is often necessary to allow your child frequent breaks from the evaluation process in order to prevent any behavioral challenges or upsets. It is usually better to schedule these breaks ahead of time rather than waiting until your child begins to show signs of being upset. We all know it can be difficult to calm a child once he's become excessively agitated. More suggestions for how to make the evaluation process a positive experience for you and your child will be provided in the "General Guidelines" section below.

The entire diagnostic evaluation might take anywhere from two to six hours, depending on the number of professionals involved. Most often, parents are provided the team's initial diagnostic impressions via an informal discussion at the end of the evaluation. A written report should be forthcoming within the next few weeks. If you do not receive a report within a month of the assessment, call the agency and prompt them to send you one.

The day of the evaluation is usually a rather tiring and difficult one for you and your child, especially if you've had to travel any distance to obtain specialized expertise. However, if conducted in a comprehensive, thorough manner with sensitivity to everyone's needs, a successful diagnostic evaluation can finally provide you with answers regarding your child's development.

What Assessment Tools Will be Used?

As you know by now, deciding whether or not a child has an ASD involves a comprehensive review of the child's developmental history and present behavioral profile, and determining whether or not specific behaviors are present. The evaluators will usually begin by going over the diagnostic criteria for an autism spectrum disorder as outlined in the *Diagnostic and Statistical Manual*, Fourth Edition (DSM-IV). (Each ASD is described in detail in Chapter Four.) At times, they may suspect a particular ASD (e.g., autistic disorder) and start with the specific diagnostic criteria for this condition. There are also a number of checklists and tests that professionals use in the evaluation process. Some of these are standardized and produce data that can be compared to the general population and others are more informal. Some diagnostic procedures are primarily interviews with parents, caretakers, and teachers, and others involve direct observation and interaction with your child. The most commonly used assessment tools, which focus specifically on whether or not a child has an autism spectrum disorder, include:

- **Autism Diagnostic Interview-Revised (ADI-R):** The ADI-R is a comprehensive, standardized set of questions posed to the parents. The test can assess individuals aged eighteen months through adulthood. Questions focus on areas such as social skills, communication abilities, and ritualistic/perseverative behaviors, such as rocking or lining up toys. The structured interview takes approximately one hour. The child's score indicates whether or not a diagnosis of an ASD is warranted. The person who administers the ADI-R needs to be trained in the procedure as well as how to score the results.

- **Autism Diagnostic Observation Schedule (ADOS):** The ADI-R and the ADOS are considered the "gold standards" for diagnosing autism spectrum disorders. In contrast to the ADI-R, the ADOS has the examiner interacting more actively with the child. Specific situations are set up and the evaluator notes how the child responds to these situations. Skill areas assessed include communication, social interactions, play skills, and ritualistic/repetitive behaviors. The ADOS can be given to preschoolers up through adults. The exam takes approximately forty-five minutes to complete.

- **Childhood Autism Rating Scale (CARS):** The CARS is a structured questionnaire that rates the severity of autistic features based on the child's behavioral and developmental profile. The examiner interviews the parents as well as observes the child's behavior directly. This system is widely used and can assess children two years and older. Each of the fifteen items, which include many of the behaviors inherent to an ASD, are scored according to a range so that the final results indicate not only if a child has autism, but also the severity of the condition. The entire procedure requires approximately forty-five minutes to complete.

- **Gilliam Autism Rating Scale (GARS):** The GARS is a checklist that can be filled out by parents, teachers, or professionals. It rates how closely a child meets the diagnostic criteria put forth by the DSM-IV. It can assess children aged three through twenty-two years. It is beneficial to have a professional review each question with the person filling out the form in order to assure that he is interpreting the questions correctly. The GARS takes approximately thirty to forty-five minutes to complete.

- **The Parent Interview for Autism (PIA):** The PIA is a questionnaire given to parents and is usually used when assessing children under six years of age, due to the nature of the questions asked. There are 118 questions in total, which tap the child's skills and behaviors across a wide range of areas including social skills, communication, sensory behaviors, and repetitive actions. The parents rate how frequently each behavior happens, providing a comprehensive review of the child's overall behavioral profile. The entire process of completing the PIA requires thirty to forty-five minutes.

Each of the tests listed above has its own set of advantages and disadvantages. As a general rule, an evaluation that includes assessment tools that involve the child responding to presented tasks (e.g., the ADOS), as well as parental questionnaires, such as the CARS and ADI-R, provides the most comprehensive understanding of the child's strengths and needs.

It is important that the professionals who diagnose your child are very experienced with the diagnostic criteria inherent to an

ASD and are able to correctly score and interpret any subsequent data. They will ask you whether or not your child has ever demonstrated a wide variety of behaviors that may indicate the presence of an autism spectrum disorder. Be as honest as you can so that the professionals can gain a full understanding of your child's development. Although it might be difficult to acknowledge some of your child's weaknesses or unusual behaviors, recognize that the examiners need this information in order to make an accurate diagnostic decision. Let the evaluators know if your child *previously* exhibited any of the behaviors, even if the behavior has since faded, as this may be relevant when making a diagnosis.

General Guidelines for Parents During a Diagnostic Evaluation

- **If you don't understand what the evaluators are asking you, be assertive and ask them to provide more explanation.** As you probably already know, the field of autism spectrum disorders has its own jargon, and at times professionals use terms without explaining their meaning. One devout mother was extremely upset when a diagnostic team mentioned that her daughter exhibited "self-stimulatory behavior." The mother's misunderstanding was obvious as she lamented to me later, "My daughter has never masturbated in her life!" If the professionals involved had been clear when using the term "self-stimulation," it would have saved this poor mother much aggravation. The moment someone uses a term or asks a question that you do not understand, ask for clarification so you can be sure you are providing accurate responses. Remember, if you misunderstand a question, you may inadvertently provide inaccurate information that can make a diagnosis more difficult to determine or lead to misdiagnosis.

■ **Ask for modifications to the testing format if you feel this will improve your child's chances of achieving valid results.** For example, if your child finds new environments or people anxiety-provoking and you question whether he will be able to perform well as a consequence, ask if you can visit the office ahead of time to introduce your child to the staff and the testing environment. As mentioned earlier, you may want to take pictures of the setting and the evaluation team and develop a "Social Story" regarding the upcoming evaluation. (See Chapter Nine for a description of "Social Stories.") If your child's attention span is limited, ask that the evaluation be broken down into realistic time segments rather than conducted all at once. Or if your child's attention span is longer at a certain time of the day, try to schedule his assessment around this schedule. If your child is comforted by your presence, it is perfectly acceptable to ask if you can remain in the room during the assessment. (Just remember that if a standardized IQ test is being administered, you are not allowed to give your child hints or even rephrase the question asked, as this will skew the results.) Bring along foods, items, drinks, or toys that are highly reinforcing for your child and have the evaluators use them to motivate your child. If you feel that your child will have significant difficulty responding successfully in an unfamiliar setting, ask the team if they are willing to conduct the assessment in your home.

■ **Bring along your child's favorite babysitter or special adult friend to run interference.** There will most likely be times during the evaluation when your child is expected to play independently while you provide information to the examiners. Many children are unable to entertain themselves in this fashion and end up distracting the parents with challenging behaviors.

If you have another adult along who can play with your child or take him on a short walk while you are being interviewed, you will be able to focus more directly on the questions being asked by the team. If no such adult is available, it may be necessary for each parent to take turns supervising the child as the alternative parent participates in the interview.

- **Try not to feel intimidated by the evaluation team.** Always remember that you know your child best and are an essential member of the evaluation team. If you are especially shy or uncomfortable in social situations, it may be helpful to bring a spouse, other family member, or even an advocate along to help you voice your concerns. If you begin to feel intimidated by the professionals during the evaluation, ask for a break, find a quiet corner and take a few deep breaths. When you feel ready, return to the evaluators and continue the assessment. The support person can also act as a note-taker as well as a shoulder to lean on if you are feeling overwhelmed, emotionally or otherwise.

- **Share the results of previous assessments with current evaluators.** Some parents worry that professionals will lean too heavily on the results of previous assessments when drawing conclusions about their child's diagnosis or intellectual abilities. They argue that the new evaluators should start with a "clean slate" when assessing their child in order to obtain the most unbiased results. While this argument is understandable, there are also valid reasons for sharing past evaluations with current assessors. Reading past reports can sometimes provide a more comprehensive review of your child's developmental history since parents may forget to mention certain information during the second assessment. Past test results also provide important data for the current evaluators, as they can compare these results with their own scores. The best professionals will be able to incorporate the results of past evaluations while recognizing that their job is to provide an objective assessment of the child's current status. Make sure to call and ask the new professionals if they have received all previous reports prior to your child's evaluation.

- **If at first you don't succeed, try, try again!** Sometimes an assessment needs to be stopped midway because of your child's escalated behaviors, passive resistance, or other factors. If this becomes necessary, make sure you arrange for a follow-up meeting with the evaluation team. Do not accept a professional's contention that your child is "untestable." If an evaluator is not able to obtain valid results from your child, find one who can. Not surprisingly, some evaluators are more adept than others at testing a child with challenging behaviors, so ask other parents and professionals who they recommend in this regard.

  If you decide to conduct a second evaluation, plan ahead so as to avoid a repeat performance. Are there ways of changing the testing situation in order to help your child succeed? If so, implement these strategies in a proactive manner so that the second assessment can be more successful. For instance, some of the preventive strategies listed earlier are useful, such as developing a Social Story or asking that the assessment take place in the home. It makes good sense to schedule an additional assessment if you feel that your child's behavior or the examiner's testing style prohibited an accurate portrayal of your child. However, if you are scheduling assessment after assessment because you disagree with the results of the evaluations, even though they are relatively consistent, you may need to consider that the results are, in fact, accurate.

- **Ask for recommendations beyond the diagnosis.** In addition to a formal diagnosis, the multidisciplinary team should provide specific recommendations about educational or treatment strategies that are indicated. If they do not do so spontaneously, parents should request this information so that they have a clear idea of their next step. Having a support person with you at the meeting to write this information down while you ask questions is useful. If you are too overwhelmed during the diagnostic evaluation to remember to ask for recommendations, it is more than acceptable to call up the diagnostic team later and ask for specific ideas. You may also want to schedule a follow-up meeting during which you can review particular questions that were left unanswered and gain insight about how to best help your child.

Getting the Diagnosis

At the end of the diagnostic evaluation, the team will usually meet with you immediately to state their conclusions about your child's diagnosis. If the team members conducted their assessments on separate occasions, a final meeting is usually scheduled so that diagnostic impressions and recommendations can be reviewed with everyone present. Parents report experiencing a wide variety of emotional reactions during this final phase of the evaluation. Whereas some parents are somewhat relieved to finally have a diagnosis to fit their child's unusual developmental profile, other parents are understandably devastated when they hear their child has an autism spectrum disorder.

Your reaction will most likely be influenced by the way the diagnosis is presented to you. If the professionals are sensitive and supportive during this discussion, parents will recognize that there is genuine reason for hope (especially if their child is young and can enter intensive early intervention services).

The professionals should allow time for the diagnosis to sink in as well as for the parents to ask any initial questions that may occur to them. If at all possible, *do not leave* until you feel that you have discussed all issues that are important to you. You may want to request to tape record the meeting so you can later review the conclusions when you're feeling more relaxed. If you still have unanswered questions, you may find it helpful to glean additional information from other sources such as the Internet, parent support groups, and books related to ASDs. More information about learning to cope with a diagnosis of ASD is covered in Chapter Eight.

Unfortunately, more often than we'd like, professionals present the diagnosis in an insensitive manner. For instance, some parents are coolly told that their child "will never function normally" or that they merely "have to adjust" to the situation. Other parents have found the evaluators to be excessively abrupt, reciting their diagnostic conclusions and then prompting the parents out the door. In their defense, most professionals do not mean to be so insensitive. For the most part, they are caring individuals who have lost track of how upsetting an ASD diagnosis can be for parents.

It is important for the diagnostic team to allow time for your questions as well as provide information about support services you can contact to begin the treatment process. As mentioned above, they should also be available to answer questions that inevitably crop up after the meeting. To assure that this can happen, identify a "point person" who will be your contact in the future. (More information about what to do if you question the evaluators' results is provided below.) You should feel comfortable calling with any questions you may have as you take the next step of planning an intervention. Remember, one of the most effective ways to decrease the stress inherent in learning your child has an ASD is to put your energy into exploring treatment options and gathering as much information as you can about the condition. The more knowledge you gain, the less you will feel overwhelmed by the situation.

Who Pays for a Diagnostic Assessment?

Unfortunately, parents have to be practical when making decisions about where they take their child for a diagnostic evaluation. Although you may want your child assessed by the most renowned experts in the field, financial considerations may limit access to these services. Many insurance companies provide at least partial payment for an initial diagnostic evaluation, so it makes sense to be informed about your insurance policy (what it will cover, what the deductible is, etc.) Gather as much information as you can so you don't wind up responsible for a large bill you assumed would be paid by insurance.

If you have an HMO (Health Maintenance Organization), again, your best bet is to become highly informed about your policy. Whenever you call your HMO, ask for the service representative's full name and extension number. Write down anything that the claims representative says in regards to payment assurances or denials and mention that you are doing so. If you feel that the claims representative does not seem sufficiently knowledgeable, ask to speak to his supervisor. Contact your referring physician or pediatrician and ensure that he has all the information necessary to support your request for the diagnostic evaluation. For example, make sure that he has the required insurance forms and that they have been filled out completely and returned to the HMO.

A frustrating trend is that insurance companies and HMOs often agree to pay for initial diagnostic evaluations but refuse to pay for subsequent treatments if your child is diagnosed with an autism spectrum disorder. According to Christopher Angelo, lawyer and the father of a boy with autism, ninety to ninety-five percent of insurance companies refuse to cover treatment for individuals with ASDs. (See Angelo's pamphlet distributed by the Autism Society of America entitled "For Our Children: A Lawyer's Guide to Insurance Coverage and a Parent's Call to Organize.") Refusal to pay is considered "justified" by the insurance company on various grounds. Some insurance companies see autism spectrum disorder as a mental health condition rather than a neurological one and therefore provide a limited amount of financial assistance. Providing any evidence you may have that refutes this contention can be helpful (e.g., send your child's EEG results if they show atypical activity). Another reason some insurance companies refuse to reimburse for treatments is that they deem the treatments "experimental," (even if repeated research has supported the interventions). Again, your best bet is to provide data that supports the treatment path you have chosen. This can be done via photocopies of journal articles related to the efficacy of the technique, records of your child's progress given the prescribed intervention, etc.

Finally, insurance companies will sometimes deny payment for services they deem "educational" and therefore the responsibility of the school system. This can apply to auxiliary or "special" services, such as speech or occupational therapies. Also, some insurance companies do not pay for the administration of IQ tests since they can be provided by schools for free. Some parents have successfully gotten previously denied insurance payments by insisting that the particular therapy addressed skills that were necessary for everyday activities (i.e., not just academic tasks). For example, you could demonstrate via documentation that your child's qualitative impairments in speech significantly hinder his ability to function within the world at large, and therefore speech therapy should be allowable under your insurance policy.

It is frequently advantageous to develop a personal connection with someone at your insurance company, whether it be your immediate representative, his supervisor, the consulting psychiatrist, etc. This is another case where being the "squeaky wheel" can work to your advantage. You want this person to be intimately familiar with your child's background and recognize who you are each time you call. You may discover that another insurance company is more open to the idea of providing funding for services to children with ASDs, and you may want to consider switching insurance carriers if this is the case. Discussing the situation with the Human Relations director at your place of employment will often help to clear up any of the questions you may have regarding insurance coverage.

If all else fails, there is always the option of seeking legal advice and support to convince your insurance carrier that the desired services should be covered. However, this decision needs to involve an objective evaluation of the financial and emotional costs such a process will require of you, and a commitment to seeing the process through to the end. If you are fully cognizant of the financial and emotional aspects of pursuing insurance payment via legal procedures but still feel that this is a route you need to take, then ask other parents and professionals for the names of local lawyers who have experience with ASDs and insurance claims.

School Assessments

Many parents rely on a diagnostic evaluation conducted by their child's school system or early intervention program, since these assessments are free of charge. If parents request that their child be evaluated, the school system is legally obligated to do so within a designated number of days. (School systems have booklets that review the educational regulations and state laws, so make sure to get a copy.) When making such a request, do so *in writing* in a dated letter that spells out your concerns specifically, as well as what professionals you feel should be involved in the evaluation. (You should keep a copy of this letter and all documents related to your child in an organized file.) School evaluations usually involve a multidisciplinary team. Members should include a school psychologist, special education teacher, speech therapist, occupational therapist, psychiatrist, and your child's classroom teacher. If the school system has not responded to your request for an evaluation within a week, contact them and ask when the evaluation will take place.

School evaluations tend to rely heavily on the administration of standardized tests, so as to produce the most objective results possible. The tests should always be clearly related to specific concerns about your child so that he is not expected to participate in unnecessary testing sessions. For example, if your child does not demonstrate any clear delays in motor skills, then a physical therapist's assessment would be unnecessary. After the school receives your request for an evaluation, they will ask you to sign a "permission to evaluate form," which should list the specific tests they are planning. If you feel that any of the tests are inappropriate, or that other tests should be considered instead, do *not* sign the form and inform the school of your reservations. Convey this message in a diplomatic manner so that you do not inadvertently damage your relationship with school personnel. Remember, these are people who will most likely be involved with your child's education for many years to come, so it is important that your relationships are cooperative and positive. Also, it may be that the school team will be able to provide a justifiable rationale as to why a particular test should be used after all.

It is not uncommon for members of the school multidisciplinary team to first observe your child in the classroom. Early intervention evaluations are also provided by school teams for children aged three to five who may not yet be attending school. Afterwards, designated members of the multidisciplinary team will conduct their own assessments of your child and then convene to discuss their findings. The multidisciplinary team members should be cognizant of the need to modify their assessment process in order to assure valid results. Feel welcome to let them know any recommendations you may have that will facilitate your child's performance during testing. For example, if your child performs best in the morning, it would be helpful if the more formal testing procedures took place before noon so that the results reflect your child's skills rather than his inability to attend in the afternoons. Inform the team members diplomatically about the ways your child communicates (e.g., signing, making certain sounds that you have learned have certain meanings, etc.) These recommendations can be provided verbally, via a written list, or in a pre-testing meeting involving you and all of the multidisciplinary team members.

The school's multidisciplinary team will later meet with you to review the results of their assessments. This meeting can take place either during school hours or afterwards and should involve all team members who have been involved in assessing your child. The team's conclusions should be compiled in a comprehensive report and you will receive a copy of this report usually within a few weeks of the meeting. As a group, you will use the results of the evaluation to determine your child's educational needs, this being the school's primary focus. Decisions may be made about appropriate classroom placement and supplemental supports such as a 1:1 aide or resource room time. Parents can be quite influential in the decision making process regarding placement and supplemental supports; in fact, many school districts invite parents to visit potential classrooms and weigh in on educational placement decisions.

After the evaluation is completed, an Individualized Education Program (IEP), or Individualized Family Service Plan (IFSP) for children under age three, will be written. The IEP details the educational objectives for a particular child, as well as methods to obtain these objectives within the coming year. These goals should be clearly linked to the child's strengths and weaknesses discovered during the evaluation process. Usually, parents want to take a week or so to digest the results of the evaluation before participating in an IEP meeting. Educational regulations, in fact, require that parents be provided this option. However, if the parents are comfortable with the results of the evaluation, they can waive the right to this waiting period and have an IEP development meeting immediately following the meeting regarding the evaluation results.

While many parents must rely on a school team for an evaluation due to financial constraints, it is still essential that they are assured the team is uniquely qualified to perform an evaluation and provide a valid diagnosis. You ought to gather information about your school district's background with autism spectrum disorders. While school districts in large metropolitan areas may have extensive experience with these children (or even have a team specifically focused on ASDs), teams in more rural sections may not have the expertise to adequately assess your child. As was discussed earlier in this chapter, it is perfectly acceptable to ask the team questions regarding their background and experience regarding ASDs in order to assess their competency in the field.

If you feel that your school district is ill-equipped to conduct a comprehensive and accurate assessment, you have the right to request that the school pay for outside experts to participate in the evaluation or conduct their own independent evaluation. You may make this request either before or after the school team has conducted their assessment. If the school refuses to comply with your appeal, you may request that a "mediation" process take place. Mediation involves a more formal meeting in which various members of the multidisciplinary team, parents, advocates, etc., sit down and attempt to finalize an agreement. If mediation efforts fail, you can ask for a "due process" hearing, which involves presenting your case (usually with a lawyer's assistance) to an objective hearing officer who will decree whether or not the school should pay for an outside evaluation. If the hearing officer agrees with your position, the school must not only pay for the evaluation but often has to pay for any lawyer fees you've accumulated in the meantime as well.

Another complicated issue that crops up when your child's evaluation takes place in his school is deciding what primary diagnosis to designate on his IEP if he has autism plus another diagnosis, such as mental retardation. This decision is influenced by the state in which you live and each state interprets the special education laws a bit differently. For example, some states allow parents and professionals to prioritize the labels on an IEP according to whichever disability is having the greatest impact on the child's learning, whereas other states mandate that certain diagnoses be listed first. You will need to determine what regulations exist in your own state. This can be accomplished by contacting your state's Department of Education or by obtaining the information on its website. Regardless of which diagnosis is listed first, you need to decide whether or not you feel that the impact of one diagnosis overrides another in terms of your child's ability to learn. While one child with autism plus mental retardation may function very well in a classroom designed primarily for children with mental retardation, another may need the specialized instruction only available in a classroom for children with autism. Discuss this issue with the multidisciplinary team and make a decision based on your child's educational needs.

There are a few disadvantages of having the school system conduct your child's diagnostic evaluation. First, as noted above, it is not uncommon for school multidisciplinary teams to have minimal experience with ASDs and therefore not be able to provide the most accurate assessment. Second, once your child has been diagnosed within the school system, educational personnel (e.g., teachers, principals, etc.) may develop certain expectations or assumptions regarding your child. In contrast, if the evaluation takes place outside of the school system (e.g., at a university-based clinic), you have complete control over which, if any, assessment results are shared with the school system. Nonetheless, many parents have found a school assessment to be a viable means of evaluating their child's diagnosis and educational needs. If this is the route you choose, remember to maintain a diplomatic, collegial relationship with the school staff. Such a positive relationship between parents and school personnel can only benefit your child through his educational experience.

What If I Don't Agree with the Results of the Diagnostic Evaluation?

Some parents wind up disappointed following a diagnostic evaluation because they are either unsure of or in total disagreement with the conclusions made by the diagnostic team. As we have discussed in earlier chapters, diagnosing ASDs is by no means a definitive process, especially when it comes to differentiating between the specific subcategories. If you feel that the results of the diagnostic evaluation are not consistent with your own perceptions of your child, it makes sense to seek a second opinion in order to make sure that you will be following the correct path when determining treatment strategies. If you do so, it is especially important to find a diagnostic team that has extensive experience in the field of autism spectrum disorders. It may be necessary to travel beyond your local community in order to do so. If the specialized setting requires significant travel time, it might be easier on everyone involved to arrive the night before and stay in a hotel. This way, everyone is fresh when you walk in the agency door for the evaluation. However, if your child finds the change in routine inherent in staying at a hotel problematic but enjoys riding in the car, it may be better to skip the hotel and give yourself plenty of travel time. You'll want to be sure you set the stage for the evaluation team to get the most accurate impression of your child.

If you have obtained a second (or even third) opinion from knowledgeable professionals and the results are consistent with the initial evaluation, it is time to look at your own agenda and consider whether you may be avoiding an unwanted truth. No parent hopes that their child has an ASD, and learning that your child is on the spectrum can be disheartening, if not heartbreaking. Some parents compare learning of the diagnosis to experiencing the death of a loved one. In other words, you are mourning the "death" of the idealized child you had anticipated. Often parents experience the phases of grief that are common after such a loss, including denial, anger, bargaining, depression, and finally acceptance. Other emotional reactions experienced by parents will be discussed in Chapter Eight.

When the diagnosis is relatively new, it is not uncommon for parents to hold onto the hope that the professionals are mistaken. If left unchecked, this can result in full-fledged denial. Although this response is understandable, you *must* remember that early intervention can make a significant difference in your child's overall progress so denying the condition is detrimental to your child in the long run.

But what if the opposite occurs? What if *you* are certain that your child has an autism spectrum disorder, but the diagnostic team tries to assure you that your fears are unfounded? When professionals tell parents that "boys are slower" and "Einstein didn't speak until he was five," this only breeds frustration and implies that parents are deliberately exaggerating their child's developmental delays. Although it is tempting to accept that nothing is wrong, if you truly feel that your child's development is atypical, it is important you continue to pursue the matter. Perhaps the first diagnostic team did not have the expertise to correctly identify an ASD and you need to seek an evaluation from a more experienced staff. Or, if your child is only a toddler, the team may have been hesitant to use one of the autism spectrum disorder diagnoses as a means of "protecting" you. A psychologist once said, "Isn't it nice that Mr. and Mrs. Smith gradually grew to recognize that their son has autism? Of course, I realized it when he was three." Such an attitude is not only patronizing, it can prevent a child from receiving appropriate treatment as early as possible.

Assessing IQ As Well As Making a Diagnosis

Depending upon the goals of the evaluation, the multidisciplinary team may also decide it makes sense to conduct standardized tests to determine your child's cognitive abilities. Although this type of comprehensive intelligence testing can be time-consuming, it is useful in providing a fuller picture of a particular child's abilities and learning styles. Considering that upwards of seventy percent of individuals with ASDs also have mental retardation, periodic IQ testing is recommended in order to evaluate the child's overall intelligence.

If intelligence testing is conducted, count on the evaluation taking place over the course of a series of meetings rather than all at once. It would be unrealistic to expect your child to participate in all of these tests over such a short period of time. In addition, many evaluators find it beneficial to break each meeting into mini-testing sessions interspersed with breaks. This way your child has the opportunity to regroup, relax with you, get a snack or drink, etc. After all, it is more important to obtain valid information and responses than it is to complete the assessment in a short amount of time.

Testing Intelligence:

The tests outlined earlier in this chapter are effective in evaluating whether or not a child has an ASD but cannot provide an overall assessment of his cognitive abilities. In order to obtain an "intelligence quotient" (IQ), a standardized IQ test needs to be administered. Before getting into the types of IQ tests that are commonly used, we'll cover some basic information about IQ tests in general.

Various types of IQ tests have been used over the decades to assess a person's overall ability to retain and use information. Although a debate continues regarding the true definition of "intelligence," most IQ tests seek to evaluate a person's ability to perceive information, process and retain that information, and respond effectively to tasks that use that information. Because of the way IQ tests are developed, a person's overall IQ should not fluctuate significantly over time. Although a person may perform more successfully as they get older (i.e., respond correctly to more tasks or questions), the overall score produced is always compared to the scores of other people the same age, so the final IQ remains relatively consistent.

It should be reiterated that traditional IQ tests can be socially and language-biased. That is, a person has to be able to communicate fairly well, understand verbal instructions, and have the social wherewithal to want to please the examiner in order to do well on these tests. Considering that most children with autism spectrum disorders have difficulties in these areas (especially when they are very young), some people believe the IQ score is probably an underestimation of the child's actual cognitive abilities. The fact that the IQs of children with ASDs under six years of age frequently fluctuate across testing sessions further supports this belief. But while this argument has merit, it should be noted that the IQ scores for children with ASDs who are six and older tend to be rather consistent through the years. This increase in accuracy is most likely due to the child's improved communication and social skills compared to when he was a toddler or preschooler. Therefore, by age six, the scores from IQ tests for children with ASDs are likely a valid representation of their intelligence.

Getting an accurate IQ for your child with an ASD can be uniquely difficult. If your child has participated in IQ testing and the results fluctuated across evaluations, there are various reasons why this might have occurred. As mentioned, your child's limitations in communication and social skills may contribute to decreased IQ scores. Also, your child's attention span and activity level can affect performance. Other factors that may influence your child's ability to respond successfully during IQ testing include changes in medication, unusual responses to sensory input, engaging in self-stimulatory behaviors, anxiety regarding being in an unfamiliar setting, and absence of functional speech.

If more than one type of IQ test is administered, the overall scores may vary. Although most IQ tests attempt to tap the same types of skills, there is not one hundred percent reliability across even the most commonly used IQ tests. A final point to be made regarding fluctuations in IQ scores is that you should assume the *highest* IQ obtained is probably the most valid representation of your child's intellectual abilities. Although there are many reasons why your child may respond incorrectly to the tasks and questions presented and therefore achieve a lower IQ, it is virtually impossible for him to "accidentally" respond correctly, resulting in an *overestimation* of his intellectual abilities.

IQ tests must be administered and interpreted by a psychologist. Administration of these tests are often part and parcel of a comprehensive evaluation rather than requiring a separate referral. Commonly used IQ tests include:

- **Wechsler Scales:** The Wechsler Scales have been administered for many decades now and are considered one of the most valid methods of assessing intelligence. The scales have been revised several times over the years. There are three Wechsler Scales: one for preschoolers, one for school aged children, and one for adults. The test is made up of subtests that tap verbal skills and nonverbal abilities. The scores on each of the subtests are compared to those of same-aged peers and an overall IQ is obtained.

As expected, children with autism spectrum disorders tend to perform better on the nonverbal subtests as compared to the verbal subtests of the Wechsler Scales. Looking at a typical Wechsler scoring pattern closely, there are certain subtests that tend to be especially difficult for children with ASDs. One, called "Comprehension," asks the child to assess various social scenarios and explain the best thing to do in those situations. Another verbal subtest that is challenging is entitled "Vocabulary" and taps the child's ability to define various words. Not surprisingly, these are frequently very difficult tasks for children with autism spectrum disorders. However, most children with ASDs perform with relative success on certain Wechsler nonverbal subtests that tap visual-motor skills (e.g., reproducing geometric block designs or puzzle completion). Therefore, it is likely that there will be clear peaks and valleys across subtest scores, with the child probably showing relatively greater visual-motor skills than social and language skills. The exception to this trend can be seen when testing children with Asperger's disorder, as these kids tend to show relative strengths in the area of verbal expression while being less adept with visual-motor skills.

The Wechsler Scales usually require at least an hour or more of direct testing. If many breaks are required, count on the testing session taking even longer or being spread across a few days.

Please note, the Wechsler Scales are revised periodically so not all the information above will remain accurate. The psychologist who tests your child will administer the most up-to-date version.

- **Stanford-Binet Intelligence Scale:** Another commonly used IQ test is the Stanford-Binet Intelligence Scale. Similar to the Wechsler Scales, the Stanford-Binet has been considered an appropriate and valid assessment tool for many decades. This test is broken down into numerous subtests, not all of which need to be administered in order to obtain a partial IQ score. Subtests tap skills in a variety of areas including memory skills, visual-performance abilities (e.g., puzzles, copying geometric designs), quantitative skills (e.g., simple addition or subtraction problems), expressive speech, and abstract reasoning. In contrast to the Wechsler Scales, there are fewer timed subtests and therefore the child is allowed additional time to respond to a given task or question. Consequently, the Stanford-Binet may provide a more accurate assessment for children who require a longer response time. As with the Wechsler Scales, the scores of children with autism spectrum disorders tend to fluctuate across the various subtests. Administration may take up to an hour or more.

- **Slosson Intelligence Test:** The Slosson Intelligence Test is commonly used when time is limited or of the essence. Administration of this test can take as little as twenty to thirty minutes. Needless to say, the information collected is less comprehensive than that obtained during administration of the Wechsler or Stanford-Binet tests. The Slosson Intelligence Test involves scoring a series of items on a yes/no scale regarding whether or not the child can do each task successfully. The items are listed in developmental order (i.e., skills expected of an infant, then those of a one-year-old, then two-year-old, etc.) Once the child fails a designated number of items, the test is discontinued and an IQ is determined. The items on the Slosson Intelligence Test become increasingly focused on communication and expressive speech as you reach the four-, five- and six-year-old items. As a consequence, the Slosson is not a particularly useful tool for assessing the intelligence of children with autism spectrum disorders.

- **Test of Nonverbal Intelligence-Third Edition (TONI-3):** Although not a true intelligence test per se, the TONI is included in this section because professionals may imply that your child's score from this test is comparable to that obtained from the Wechsler or Stanford-Binet Scales. The TONI requires the individual to use nonverbal problem-solving skills (e.g., determining which geometric design completes a given pattern). Since there are no verbal instructions or requirements for verbal responses, the TONI is often seen as a viable alternative IQ test for children with ASDs. Although the final score is termed an "IQ," the problem-solving skills tapped by the TONI are much narrower than the wide variety of abilities tapped by more comprehensive IQ tests, such as the Wechsler or the Stanford-Binet, and therefore the resulting score should not be interpreted as an actual IQ, per se.

Is an IQ Score Enough to Determine Mental Retardation?

If your child shows notable fluctuations across subtest scores, and in fact displays age-appropriate skills in certain areas, a diagnosis of mental retardation may not be appropriate. This is true even if the overall IQ obtained indicates mental retardation (an IQ of seventy or below). Any interpretation of IQ test results needs to take into consideration the child's specific strengths and deficits and any possible causes for poor performance. The evaluator should note in his report any extenuating circumstances that may have affected the child's performance (e.g., distractions from the environment), as well as any accommodations he made to the testing process (e.g., pairing correct responses with edible rewards). As a general rule, the examiner should finish the report by citing whether or not the test results appear to be a valid representation of the child's actual cognitive abilities.

It is important to note that an IQ score alone cannot determine whether or not an individual has mental retardation. In addition to an IQ score of less than seventy, a person must show significant delays or deficits in what is termed "adaptive behavior" to be diagnosed as having mental retardation. Adaptive behavior refers to skills that are necessary for performing everyday tasks and routines, such as self-help skills, communicating needs, engaging in activities that require fine and gross motor skills, completing home chores, and developing relationships with others. Research has consistently shown that children with ASDs, especially those with significant cognitive impairments, tend to exhibit delays in adaptive behavior skills that can limit their ability to effectively perform daily tasks. Although children with ASDs whose intellectual abilities are in the average to above average range may show age-appropriate skills in certain adaptive areas (e.g., self-help, motor skills), they often continue to display deficits in the areas of social and communication skills.

There are various checklists for assessing adaptive behavior skills, which can be administered by a variety of individuals including case managers, social workers, and psychologists. As is the case with IQ tests, these tests are often part and parcel of a comprehensive evaluation and don't require that parents get a separate referral. The most common adaptive behavior scales are:

- **Vineland Adaptive Behavior Scales:** The Vineland is a well-accepted tool for assessing a person's adaptive behavior skills. The assessment involves an evaluator conducting a semi-structured interview of parents, teachers, or other individuals who are well acquainted with the child's abilities. The questionnaire is divided into various skill areas, such as communication, socialization, and daily living skills. The scores are compared with those obtained from same-aged peers and the child's overall profile is examined. The Vineland requires approximately an hour of interviewing time.

- **AAMR's Adaptive Behavior Scales: School (ABS:S):** For children who are significantly less advanced, the ABS:S is a helpful tool in providing a more detailed assessment of their overall adaptive skills compared to the Vineland. Similar to the Vineland Adaptive Behavior Scales, the ABS:S involves a semi-structured interview in which an adult who is familiar with the child scores the child's abilities across a wide range of adaptive areas. The ABS:S takes approximately an hour to complete. The scores can then be compared to either same-aged peers who show typical development, or to same-aged peers functioning within the mentally retarded range. If your child's adaptive abilities are similar to a same-aged child with mental retardation and he has received an IQ score of less than seventy, then it is likely he may have mental retardation as well as an ASD.

Why Determine If My Child Has Mental Retardation As Well As an ASD?

As mentioned earlier, the primary purpose of any diagnosis is to help you design an appropriate treatment plan. If your child has both mental retardation plus an ASD, the specific teaching strategies used and classroom placement may very well be different than if your child has autism but functions intellectually within the average or above average range. The specific support services your child may require will likely be more intensive if he has mental retardation as well as an ASD. The presence of a dual diagnosis helps you have a better understanding of your child's prognosis and more realistic expectations, for the overall progress of a child with both mental retardation and autism is generally slower than that of a child with an autism spectrum disorder alone.

Concluding Comments

Participating in a diagnostic evaluation is a day parents will never forget, regardless of the final conclusions. Hopefully your experiences will be relatively positive as far as the professionals involved being comprehensive, knowledgeable, and sensitive to your emotions. Always remember that the primary reason to diagnose your child is to determine appropriate treatment and education, so this should be your focus following the diagnosis. Also, remember that not all children with ASDs are the same and your child is an individual with his own personality and future. Try to avoid becoming immersed in other parents' "war stories" or making assumptions about your child's developmental potential. Remain hopeful, an emotion that is more than warranted considering the treatment strategies that will be described in Chapter Nine.

Parents Speak

The early diagnostic process with our psychologist was a wonderful and enlightening experience. She was very helpful. She discussed everything with us and allowed us to ask questions and cry when we needed to.

෧෨

After finally admitting to ourselves that something was wrong with our three-year-old son, we went to a neurologist, who after ten minutes of observation, very matter-of-factly said, "He's autistic." He handed us a pamphlet on autism and told us to come back in several weeks. The forty-five minute car ride home made for one of the longest, saddest days in our marriage. We were crying, but didn't even really know why. In hindsight, I wish I had demanded the doctor give us more time and attention; at least the courtesy to let us process the diagnosis.

A multidisciplinary team in the hospital gave Paul a developmental full scale evaluation. Their prognosis was rather grim and institutional care was their ultimate prediction. They reviewed the evaluation with us and very quickly figured out that my husband wasn't buying into it. The team was determined to make him face the diagnosis. They wanted him to say the words, "He's autistic." My husband never did say those words that day, and he rarely does to this day (thirteen years later). He refuses to voice limitations, he sees the reality of Paul's skills and accepts him for who he is, but always keeps the "hope door" wide open.

The personnel at the pediatric rehab center where our daughter was diagnosed were attuned to autistic behavior issues and did not become frustrated or angry if a test could not be completed for an evaluation. I think I would get more frustrated and upset when this happened than they would. They were very supportive. They even offered the names of support groups and parents we could call when we needed a boost or a question answered.

∽

I have read about the "diagnose and dump" scenario that many parents experience with professionals, and unfortunately, I felt it first hand. My initial feelings of shock and disbelief about the diagnosis turned to anger, mostly at the way the situation was handled. Honestly, my feelings of anger were tied to wanting to kill the messenger, and not wanting to have a child with autism. I later thanked this pediatrician for bringing my daughter's "autistic qualities" to my attention so that I could get her help, but I also let him know that his uncaring manner made the process so much harder for me.

The Maritti Family

When first told that their son, Timmy, had pervasive developmental disorder-not otherwise specified (PDD-NOS), Donna and Brian Maritti felt confused and overwhelmed. They had never even heard of the term before, and now they felt immense pressure to find appropriate treatment for Timmy. The professionals from the diagnostic team had provided reams of literature, websites, and even the phone number for a local support group; however, the Marittis did not have the energy to follow through on any of these recommendations. For the first few months after Timmy's diagnosis, they felt as if they were in a daze, unable to discuss their feelings even with each other. "I was afraid that she would fall apart if I brought up the subject," Brian said. As for Donna, she interpreted Brian's silence as disinterest. "It felt like I was the only one who cared about Timmy. I spent many nights feeling alone and crying myself to sleep."

Over time, the Marittis have come to realize they are each other's best ally in the fight to help Timmy. Under the guidance of a family counselor, Donna and Brian have begun discussing their emotions with each other and working as a team. They've divided the tasks necessary to gain a better understanding of PDD-NOS and Timmy's needs. Since Donna enjoys reading, she has taken it upon herself to read many of the books on the reference list provided by the diagnostic team. Brian's notable people skills led him to network with local parents and professionals. Although they continue to be concerned about Timmy's developmental differences, they now have a sense of *mutual focus. As they begin to develop appropriate and effective treatment strategies as well as understand the local special education system, they feel less overwhelmed.* As Brian notes, "*Knowledge is power!*"

The Maritti's experience is quite typical of a family whose child has recently been diagnosed with an autism spectrum disorder. Parents, siblings, and extended family members find themselves on an emotional roller coaster, especially in the early days, weeks, and months after diagnosis. If your child has recently been diagnosed with an autism spectrum disorder, the following emotions will almost certainly sound familiar.

Common Emotional Reactions

Shock/Disbelief

As was the Maritti's experience, many parents report feeling shocked and overwhelmed when their child is first diagnosed with an ASD. Most people have scant knowledge of autism and little reason to anticipate that their own child may wind up with this disorder. Feelings of shock are more common if a child is still quite young and her parents have not yet noticed development differences. Even if parents have recognized their child's developmental delays (e.g., absence of speech), they may have assumed she was "going through a phase" that she would soon grow out of. But a diagnosis of an ASD usually implies a lifelong condition, thus putting an abrupt and unpleasant end to this kind of thinking. On the other hand, if parents have been questioning their child's developmental differences for months or even years, getting a diagnosis may result in a feeling of relief or validation.

Denial

It is quite natural for parents to respond to feelings of shock and disbelief by denying that a problem exists. They may underemphasize their child's behavioral differences or insist that the diagnostic team made a mistake. As mentioned in Chapter Seven, it is perfectly reasonable to arrange for a second or even third opinion to assure that the diagnosis is correct. But take care not to spend undue time or money going from professional to professional, hoping you will eventually hear someone say your child's development is fine. This will only hurt you and your child in the long run.

Depression/Sadness

It is absolutely normal to feel depressed when faced with the fact that your child has an autism spectrum disorder. As noted earlier, some parents go through a period of "mourning" for the loss of the child they imagined they'd have. Feelings of sadness are almost unavoidable for parents of newly diagnosed children and you should not beat yourself up for having these feelings. *Allow yourself time* to adjust to the fact that your child has an ASD rather than putting pressure on yourself to hurry up and accept it.

Sometimes this sadness develops into more intense feelings of depression and can require professional support. Symptoms of clinical depression include loss of interest in previously preferred activities, frequent crying episodes, changes in sleeping or appetite, lethargy, thoughts of death or dying, or even suicidal urges. It is common for parents of newly diagnosed children to show some or even all of these symptoms initially; however, if the symptoms continue over a period of a few months, it is likely that clinical depression is present. If so, professional assistance in the form of psychotherapy or antidepressant medication may be warranted. Also, as with the Marittis, it is essential for spouses to work together on adjusting to the diagnosis rather than trying to resolve the inherent emotional upheaval on their own.

> Allow yourself time to adjust to the fact that your child has an ASD rather than putting pressure on yourself to hurry up and accept it.

Anger

It is not uncommon for parents of newly diagnosed children to feel angry and frustrated. You may ask yourself, "Why?," only to be frustrated when told that the underlying cause(s) for the majority of children with autism spectrum disorders is rarely determined. You may feel that having a child with an ASD is "unfair" and dwell on the injustice of the situation. One advantage of angry feelings is that, in contrast to depression, people often feel energized when angry. Try using this energy for constructive activities, like gathering information or advocating for services for your child.

Blaming Yourself or Others

Some parents respond to learning that their child has an autism spectrum disorder by blaming others such as their spouse or their obstetrician, even though there is no scientific proof indicating that errors during delivery are linked to ASDs. Parents should be careful not to focus their energy on blaming others, as this ultimately does little to help their child and can be emotionally draining. If you find yourself blaming your spouse (e.g., if there seems to be a genetic link on his or her side of the family), remember that any genetic input was outside of your spouse's control and therefore not malicious or deliberate. Remember that your spouse is equally upset regarding the fact that your child has an ASD and placing blame will only make matters worse.

In addition to blaming others, parents tend to look towards themselves and their own behavior when assigning blame. They may worry if they experimented with drugs as an adolescent or drank alcohol during pregnancy. They may perceive having a child with an ASD as a sign that they've "failed" as a parent. Remember, there is no proof that parental behaviors, either in regards to prenatal or postnatal care, are to blame for the presence of an autism spectrum disorder. Blaming yourself will only lead to increased feelings of depression and worthlessness. If a tendency to blame yourself or others seems excessive and overwhelming to you, it may prove worthwhile to seek professional help.

Guilt

One of the most frequently experienced feelings reported by parents of children with ASDs is guilt. You may feel you've somehow caused your child's developmental differences. Or you may feel you aren't doing enough for your child. Or maybe not the *right* things. Professionals may inadvertently promote this reaction by putting undue pressure on you about what programs you should be implementing at home. Family members and friends sometimes offer unsolicited advice about how to raise your child, also contributing to these guilty feelings.

Parents may also feel guilty about missed early intervention services if they did not seek professional help until their child was five years or older. Considering how important early intervention can be for these children, you may feel you have "failed" your child if you didn't push for these services early on or got a diagnosis too late. Remember, it's always 'better late than never' to organize services for your child. For the most part, guilt is an insidious emotion that can be highly destructive. Therefore, you ought to have realistic expectations of yourselves and focus on the many ways you have already helped your child and what you can do *now*.

Fear Regarding the Future

Parents often experience fear, especially about the future, in reaction to the news about their child. You may wonder if your child will ever be a part of a regular classroom, get married, have children, or be able to hold a job. Unfortunately, these types of questions are usually impossible to answer, especially when your child is very young. If there are other conditions involved such as mental retardation, the overall prognosis can seem more grim. However, there is genuine reason for hope that she will make significant progress given specialized services.

As parents, you may feel some or all of these emotions during the course of adjusting to your child's new diagnosis. You can anticipate that these feelings will eventually fade in intensity and frequency over time. However, at least some of these emotions will probably recur to some extent. That is, you may again experience periods of your life when you feel overwhelmed, saddened, guilty, etc., even after your child has grown into adulthood. Some parents report that their emotions tend to be most intense upon first hearing the diagnosis, when their child reaches age twenty-one, and if their child moves out of the home into a supervised setting.

Having a child with an autism spectrum disorder can be fraught with difficult emotions. However, between these difficult experiences will be many reasons for celebration and happiness. Parents of children with ASDs often appreciate the little accomplishments that their child achieves—accomplishments that they may have otherwise taken for granted. For example, one family rejoiced when their child was finally potty trained at age eight. Bigger accomplishments are possible as well, as reflected by the family that always carries multiple photographs of their son at his bar mitzvah. Remember that the great majority of children with ASDs eventually gain a wide variety of skills and show notable progress over the years. Taking the time to notice and appreciate these accomplishments will facilitate a smoother adjustment.

Factors That May Affect Your Emotional Reactions

Various factors may influence the kind of emotional reaction you have when you hear that your child has an autism spectrum disorder. First, *your own personality* will affect how you respond. For example, if in the past you have responded to hardships by being stoic and focused, this will probably be your reaction upon learning your child's diagnosis. In contrast, if your personality leans towards emotional upheavals and feelings of anxiety, you may find the diagnosis more difficult to accept. There is no "right" or "wrong" way to react, and cramming your emotions down deep serves you no better than screaming about them. No matter what your tendency, it may prove worthwhile to seek therapy in order to help you come to terms with the diagnosis and decrease negative feelings.

Another factor that will influence your reaction is the *severity of your child's condition*. If your child's development is extremely delayed, or she demonstrates highly problematic behavior such as self-injury, physical aggression, or sleep disturbances, adjusting to the diagnosis can be especially difficult. You may find yourself overwhelmed by the day-to-day challenges and therefore have little time or energy to direct towards your own emotional needs. Behavioral parent training, which can provide specific strategies to teach skills and decrease challenging behaviors and is often provided by local school or state agencies, can be a good way to get a handle on these challenging behaviors. Chapter 9 will provide more information about behavioral techniques used with children with ASDs.

A third area that can greatly influence parents' responses to this life change is the *amount of support available* within their family and community. Single parents without any extended family members nearby usually feel more overwhelmed than married couples who have numerous family and community supports. It can also be more difficult for the "stay-at-home" spouse as compared to the husband or wife who works out of the home and is therefore able to find some respite. In any situation, it is essential that parents actively seek out respite, advocacy assistance, as well as advice from friends, family, and local agencies. Also, talking to other parents of children with ASDs helps you feel less alone and overwhelmed. Local agencies can usually provide a list of support groups in your area. Some parents find it more practical to make connections on the Internet via chat rooms and list-serves that are specific to ASDs. After all, no one can fully understand your emotions or concerns as well as another parent who has experienced similar feelings.

The *amount of knowledge you have* about ASDs and effective interventions will inevitably affect your emotional reactions to the diagnosis. As Brian Maritti noted, "Knowledge is power!" Parents with recently diagnosed children with ASDs often feel at a loss, and this helplessness can lead to feeling emotionally over-whelmed. The more you learn about ASDs, the less helpless you will feel, and the more energy and motivation you'll have to learn even more. Read books, access ASD websites on the Internet, and ask a lot of questions of professionals and fellow parents so you can be as well-informed as possible.

Searching for "Cures"

Parents of newly-diagnosed children are especially suscep-tible to buying into unproven "cure-alls" promoted by less than ethical professionals in the field. As a general rule, it is important for parents to be cautious before accepting any claims regarding "cures" or unproven treatment methodologies. At the very least, some of these proposed "cures" can be very expensive and at worst can potentially harm your child. Some parents decide to try a given approach because "it couldn't hurt," when in fact this may not be true. For example, something that seems "natural," such as provid-ing high dosages of vitamins to your child, can lead to side effects such as nausea and muscle weakness. As discussed in Chapter Nine, there are numerous interventions that have been supported by sci-entific research and are usually the best bet for children with au-tism spectrum disorders. Although it is more than understandable that parents feel frantic in their search for the most effective inter-vention possible and willing to try almost anything, especially given the emphasis on early intervention, it's essential you keep a clear and objective perspective during this time.

Practical Issues

Breaking the News

Once your child has been diagnosed with an autism spec-trum disorder, as parents, you'll need to make numerous practical decisions. Beginning with, *"Who should know about the diagnosis and who should receive copies of the evaluation report?"* While some parents do not wish to share the results of the evaluation with other people, most recognize it is in their child's best interest to inform all appropriate parties. It's beneficial to distribute the evaluation report to all relevant professionals in your child's life, such as her pediatrician, neurologist, speech therapist, and school staff. It is useful to schedule a meeting to review the report with others rather than merely sending it off through the mail. Sharing the report may reveal funding possibilities for treatment or respite services.

More often than not, if your child is already attending school, the school personnel will not be surprised that an outside evaluator has determined your child has developmental differences. Reviewing the results of the evaluation can help the school staff develop a more effective Individualized Education Program (IEP), which in turn will most likely improve your child's school performance. If your child does not yet have an IEP, contact your local school system and request a meeting to discuss the results of the diagnostic evaluation as well as your child's educational needs. Within a week or so, the school district's special education team should meet with you to start the IEP process. Often, school districts conduct their own evaluation of the child and then the team (including parents) develops an IEP, which notes educational goals as well as methods that will be implemented to meet those objectives within the coming year. *Negotiating the Special Education Maze: A Guide for Parents and Teachers*, 3rd ed. (Anderson, Chitwood, & Hayden, 1997), is a useful tool for parents during this process.

Similarly, most parents decide to share the fact that their child has an autism spectrum disorder with relatives and close friends. Discussing your concerns and feelings with people who can support you in a nurturing manner is almost invariably beneficial. Of course, there is no easy way to break the news to family and friends. Often, others have had concerns about your child and may have even questioned the possibility of an ASD, but have been hesitant to share their concerns with you. Usually, it is easiest to broach the topic slowly by making a statement such as, "As you know, we've been concerned about Bobby's development." Then state the facts as you know them. Considering that most people in the general population have little knowledge about ASDs, you will be faced with many questions you may not be able to answer on your own. It may be useful to ask family members and friends to gather information as a joint effort and then meet as a group to discuss what you have learned. Also, it may be beneficial to have family members or close friends attend IEP meetings or follow up meetings with the diagnostic team to give them a chance to learn more about ASDs and provide support to you.

Having Further Testing Done

"Should more extensive testing be conducted?" It is not uncommon for parents and professionals to pursue further testing in order to rule out any medical concerns that may affect their children. For example, a neurologist may recommend an EEG or MRI to determine if your child has any underlying neurological problems, such as seizures. As discussed in Chapter Three, genetic testing may also be warranted, especially if there seems to be a familial pattern of developmental differences or if you are planning to have additional children. This is particularly important if your child has been diagnosed with fragile X syndrome, which can be passed down to future children because of abnormalities in the mother's genetic makeup. Some parents have found it helpful to have their child tested for allergies, as these may affect her learning and behavioral profile.

When deciding whether or not to pursue additional testing, parents should weigh the potential benefits and disadvantages of such tests. Are there potential negative side effects of the test? For example, would the test protocol be particularly difficult or tiring for your child? Are the answers provided by a specific test relevant and important (e.g., if parents are not planning on having any more children, is genetic testing necessary?)? Would the results of a particular test lead directly to treatment options? If so, any disadvantages of the test may be outweighed by the potential benefits of a new intervention.

Seeking Information

Another question often asked by parents of newly diagnosed children is, *"Where do I get more information and assistance?"* Although a competent evaluation team should provide you with specific resources to assist you in taking the next steps toward knowledge and treatment, unfortunately, there are times when you are merely given a diagnosis and sent on your way. If this is your experience, call the diagnostic team and solicit specific recommendations. It can be beneficial to identify one of the diagnostic team members as your "point person" and relay any questions you may have through her. However, if your questions are not being adequately answered using this route, you may need to talk to each professional separately.

Local chapters of the Autism Society of America (ASA) can also be a starting point for parents, as can parent support groups. As mentioned earlier, local social service agencies often have lists of support groups in the area that may be able to help you. Although talking to other parents can be valuable, remember their experiences will not necessarily mirror what is in store for you and your child's future. Schools and state mental health/mental retardation agencies can frequently provide reading lists and information regarding local resources. Although the Internet can be a viable means of gathering information, keep in mind that this information is less stringently monitored and may include questionable ideas. The Resource Guide provided at the end of this book will further steer you in the direction of information and assistance.

Setting Goals

A final practical issue that parents need to address is *prioritizing goals* for their child. Initially, parents often feel an urgent need to address all their concerns at once and wind up spreading themselves and their child too thin in the process. It is more valuable for parents to prioritize their goals and focus on each one in a systematic fashion. It may prove worthwhile to make a list of your goals for your child and then highlight the ones that are of utmost concern. Ones you may place at the top of the list include addressing medical issues, behaviors that place the child or others in danger, sleep disturbances, and development of communication skills. Remain realistic as you develop and prioritize your goals so that you don't feel overwhelmed. It's a good idea to ask your child's Early Intervention team or school staff to help make these decisions.

General Recommendations

- **Develop a file that includes all evaluations, recommendations, handwritten notes, data, etc. related to your child's condition.** Organize the file in such a way that information is easily accessible. You can refer to these records as needed during meetings, phone calls, and other planning sessions.

- **Develop realistic, but *respectful*, goals for your child.** While it is essential to recognize your child's developmental differences, it is disrespectful to assume she cannot rise to realistic expectations. For example, do not assume that you must merely accept behavioral challenges because your child "does not know any better"; instead, obtain assistance in developing effective and consistent behavioral interventions that you can use to both decrease unwanted behaviors as well as increase desirable ones.

- As Brian Maritti stated in the opening scenario, "Knowledge is power." **The more you learn about ASDs, the better equipped and more assured you will be that**

your child is receiving the most effective treatment. Also, knowledge decreases feelings of stress, helplessness, and being overwhelmed.

■ Keep in mind that there will be many unanswered questions, especially in regard to the cause(s) underlying autism spectrum disorder as well as your child's long-term future. Although this can be frustrating, **do your best to accept that there will be some "unknowns."**

■ There are times when parents resent needing to "teach the professionals." Unfortunately, the majority of school and medical professionals have little experience with autism spectrum disorders. Although it is important to seek out professionals who *have* experience in this field, there will be instances when you need to **be vocal in describing the disorder and advocating for your child's needs** to less experienced staff. It may be helpful to imagine yourself as an advocate for all children with autism spectrum disorders by increasing others' knowledge.

■ As discussed, it is not uncommon for parents to initially feel overwhelmed when their child is diagnosed with an ASD. It can be difficult to process and retain information when in this emotional state. Therefore, it may be beneficial to **go back and review information in order to assure complete comprehension**. It is acceptable to reconnect with the evaluation team in order to ask (or even repeat) questions that you still have. It is advantageous to write down the information that is provided in order to have a reference later on. Some parents find it useful to tape record meetings so that they can play the tape later to clarify any aspects of the discussion.

- Each family member will respond to hearing the diagnosis in their own way. While some family members find it helpful to discuss the issue with others, some may feel the need to spend long hours in quiet reflection. There is no "right" way to respond and it is unrealistic to expect everyone will respond the same way that you did. Of utmost importance is the need to **communicate and support one another.** Honest discussions should include not only how you can help other family members, but how *you* can be supported by them as well.

- If your child's school system conducted the diagnostic evaluation, two steps in the decision-making process regarding your child's education usually take place. First, the results of the evaluation will be reviewed and discussed. Second, an IEP will be developed, which will include your child's educational needs as well as recommended classroom placement. It is generally beneficial to **hold two distinct meetings rather than complete both of these processes during one session.** Separate meetings allow you time to digest the information, investigate options, and increase your knowledge about ASDs prior to making any firm decisions about classroom placement or your child's educational needs.

- It is common for parents of newly diagnosed children to over-focus on their child with an ASD and become consumed with her needs. This response is understandable and almost inevitable in the short term. Try to remember to **balance everyone's needs within the family (including your own) in order to decrease the possibility of parental burn-out and sibling resentment.**

- **Although having a child with an autism spectrum disorder is not likely your choice for a life experi-**

ence, it can nonetheless be a path filled with in-sight and rewards. As mentioned earlier, the joy experienced when your child accomplishes a skill that would be taken for granted in a typically developing child can be extremely rewarding. Also, your child's unique view of the world can teach you things about your own life. *A Will of His Own: Reflections on Parenting a Child with Autism* (Harland, 2002) is a wonderful collection of essays that realistically explores one mother's experience raising her son with autism.

- **Remember that your child is a child *first*, and a child with an autism spectrum disorder *second*.** Although the diagnosis can be overwhelming at times, recognize that your child is a unique person with her own remarkable qualities. Make lists of your child's special attributes (e.g., a great smile, perseverance when faced with obstacles, etc.) Try to lead as "normal" a family life as possible, such as planning family vacations and going out to dinner together. Although these activities may require a bit of creative planning and even additional helping hands from friends or extended family members, they are important and worth the effort.

- Last but not least, **remember to allow yourself time to digest the fact that your child has an autism spectrum disorder.** Do not make any rash decisions about what to do next until you have had time to fully process the situation and gain additional information.

Parents Speak

Hearing the diagnosis for the first time was very emotional. It is still an emotional roller coaster for me on a daily basis. I wonder what life will be like for my son at age twenty-one or

age forty. There is so much uncertainty. *I want to protect him,
but yet, want him to be independent and functioning at his
maximum potential so he can be happy. I don't think I'll ever
get off this emotional roller coaster.*

⚲

*No one wants their child, let alone both their children, to
have any health problems or delays. We did everything hu-
manly possible to bring them into the world healthy. To find
out two years down the road that something was wrong was
such heartache.*

⚲

*I hear some people say they felt relieved when their child was
diagnosed with autism. Alexandra's diagnosis brought only
fear and worry for me, not relief. I kept focusing on her future
and what that would be like, and if I had the emotional
strength to deal with everything that would come our way.*

⚲

*I never really accepted the diagnosis until he was six. At first,
I tried to do everything I could to show that my son was not
autistic. I worked with all the services on improving his
shortcomings. I was hoping that Early Intervention would be
so effective that he would no longer carry a label. That did
not happen, and now I can honestly say that I am comfortable with his diagnosis. I no longer obsess about the future,
but take each day at a time. I also have more confidence in my
abilities to parent a child with special needs, and this makes
all the difference.*

⚲

Support from other parents was, and still is, essential to our well-being. We have been able to get great ideas from other parents and gain the perspective that we are not in this alone.

Our sons' diagnoses hit us hard. I have a twenty-year-old autistic, severely mentally challenged nephew. I know what my sister's life has been like because of her son. My heart hurt for all that my nephew and my boys would not experience. Our goal is to keep our children happy and safe. We will pursue all reasonable avenues in helping them reach their maximum potential.

Early on, I remember one night when I was so tired and had no one to turn to. So, I called up Andrew's psychologist and left a message: "This is Heather. I know it's four o'clock in the morning, and I know you aren't in the office, but I need to talk to someone. Andrew has been turning lights on and off all night. He won't sleep. I'm exhausted and so frustrated! I know you're not there, I just needed to tell someone who would understand. Thanks for listening."

Educate family members not to undermine your chosen teaching strategies. Tolerance and acceptance by all members is one of the best ways to move forward.

9 | **Treatment**

The Andrews Family

Although she had only obtained a high school degree, for all her extensive research into treatment strategies for children with autism spectrum disorders, Grace Andrews felt she deserved multiple educational degrees. By the time her son, Paul, was three years old, Grace had attended numerous conferences and workshops related to autism. By the time Paul was five, Grace could tell you the address of every autism-related website and was overseeing Paul's home-based Applied Behavior Analysis (ABA) program. Grace earned a reputation for being up-to-date on the latest and most effective treatment techniques. Within a few years, she was speaking at local workshops and was even writing a book about her experiences as a single mom raising a child with an autism spectrum disorder.

Because of her skills and reputation, other parents often ask Grace her opinion about specific treatment strategies and educational approaches. Wisely, Grace recognizes that all children with ASDs are individuals and therefore treatment packages must be personalized. However, she also realizes that there are certain standards by which to judge whether or not a particular approach makes sense. She stresses that parents should not leap onto treatment bandwagons without thoroughly researching their underlying strategies and determining whether or not they apply to their child's needs and developmental profile. She also emphasizes the need to rely on data derived from comprehensive research studies, rather than accepting a few anecdotal reports as proof of a given strategy's effectiveness.

While she remains open-minded to new ideas, Grace has seen many "cures" come and go over the years and is wary of anyone touting an approach that would cure all children with autism spectrum disorders. Other parents appreciate Grace's advice and feel she is able to empathize with their need to balance objectivity with the pressure to help their child **now**.

Having a child with an autism spectrum disorder compels parents to learn more about the topic than they imagined possible. More than a few parents have become experts in the field after spending long hours gathering information, attending conferences, and weighing the various treatment options reviewed in the research literature. Such dedication is admirable and undoubtedly will increase your child's opportunities to receive the most effective interventions available. However, it can be difficult to effectively assess the many approaches to treating ASDs. The proponents of each approach often insist that their intervention is the only one that should be considered. Since this is a highly individualized process, you must develop a method for evaluating each intervention and determining whether or not it will work for your son or daughter. This chapter will review the most up-to-date treatment techniques for ASDs and set you on a path to making an informed decision about which approaches make the most sense for your family.

How do you know if a given treatment strategy makes sense for your child? First of all, as a general rule, do not adopt any approach that does not provide some degree of scientific proof of its effectiveness. Anecdotal evidence (i.e., descriptions regarding the positive effect the treatment has on only a few children) is much less convincing than a careful scientific study involving a large group of children and careful manipulation of specific intervention techniques. If you decide to try a given treatment, allow a sufficient amount of time to expect results (e.g., a month or two), but do not prolong your commitment to a strategy that has shown few positive effects.

Keep in mind that you will *want* to see success, especially if you have put forth lots of money or energy for the treatment.

Therefore, you may think you see progress when in fact none has occurred. In order to assure that your evaluation of a given strategy is objective and unbiased, it is valuable to systematically keep track how your child is progressing. For example, keep a running tally of how many words he can say in one sentence or how often he has a tantrum. Focus on the skills or behaviors that are supposed to be affected by the treatment strategy. For example, if a technique professes to improve social skills, count how many times your child initiates an interaction with others or maintains eye contact. Comparing these data to those collected *before* the start of a new treatment program can give you a better idea of whether or not the treatment is truly effective. So, obtaining a baseline of your child's behavior prior to beginning a new treatment program is an excellent idea.

Finally, keep in mind that all children go through phases. You might find that a strategy that used to be effective for your child suddenly stops working. By continually collecting and reviewing this kind of information, you will be able to recognize when a change in treatment techniques is warranted.

Why Is Early Intervention Important?

Research indicates that implementing treatment as early as possible improves the overall prognosis for children with autism spectrum disorders (Harris & Gill-Weiss, 1998). Studies have shown there is a period of time, before the age of five, when a child's brain is rapidly developing. During this time, healthy parts of the brain are often able to compensate (e.g., take over "jobs") for the areas that are impaired. In fact, certain research has shown that some children with ASDs who are provided intensive direct instruction, such as Discrete Trial Instruction (DTI), prior to age five, are eventually able to be included in typi-

> Research indicates that implementing treatment as early as possible improves the overall prognosis for children with autism spectrum disorders (Harris & Gill-Weiss, 1998).

cal classrooms. The incidence of this happening for children who begin treatment after five years of age is much lower. At the same time, this is not to imply that parents should give up or forego treatment if their child has not received intensive intervention prior to age five; in fact, many of the techniques described below are highly effective for older children and even adults with ASDs.

Educational Setting Options

Most children with autism spectrum disorders receive treatment in specialized schools, classrooms, or clinics. Each state has its own special education terminology, policies, and procedures, so it is important for you to become familiar with your own local regulations. Generally speaking, special education classrooms tend to be organized according to children's abilities and needs. Often, there are specialized classes specifically for children with ASDs; however, this does not mean that this type of setting is the most appropriate for all children with this diagnosis. Some children with ASDs are fully or partially included in regular education classrooms. The treatment and education of every child with an ASD should be individualized. As you now know, schools are required to develop an Individualized Education Plan (IEP) for all children with special educational needs, and the IEP outlines the children's specific goals as well as methods to achieve these goals. The IEP will drive decisions about which type of classroom makes the most sense for each child.

Specialized Schools

Specialized schools, which provide education specifically for students with ASDs or similar disorders, exist across the nation. Often, these schools are small and can provide more intensive teaching than public school systems. Of special benefit is the fact that the teachers are specifically trained in the education of children with ASDs. The major disadvantage of these settings is that the students usually have little opportunity to be around typically developing peers and therefore lose the benefit of these peers modeling appropriate social and language skills. However, for many students (especially those with significant needs or behavioral challenges), a specialized school is the best option.

Specialized Classrooms

Most school districts provide special education *classrooms* developed to provide services to children with ASDs or other learning difficulties. As a general rule, the students in these classes are grouped according to diagnosis or level of intellectual functioning. These classrooms are usually housed in public schools so that the students with ASDs have an opportunity to interact with typically developing peers either informally (e.g., in the cafeteria, on the playground) or formally (e.g., participating in music class with a regular education class).

Home-based ABA Programs

Although most children with ASDs are educated in specialized classrooms, there has been a recent trend to provide intervention in other settings, such as the child's home, especially when the child is very young (Maurice, 1996). For example, as will be described later in this chapter, many home programs exist around the country that involve 1:1 ABA (Applied Behavior Analysis) instructors coming to the home for up to 40 hours per week, providing intensive teaching to young children with ASDs. Parents may feel this type of home program can be too intrusive, and advocate for the same intensive program to be implemented outside of the home (e.g., within a specialized preschool setting). Whether in the home or in a specialized classroom, research shows that these types of programs can be highly beneficial and lead to significant positive results.

Other parents find it beneficial to personally home-school their child with an ASD so that they can have more control over what their child is learning and what techniques are being implemented. Intervention implemented in the home is especially advantageous for a young child because he is likely most comfortable in the home environment and therefore treatment effects can be maximized. However, instructing a child at home requires a significant commitment of time and energy on the part of the parents and this needs to be considered before deciding to go this route.

Inclusion

Another trend gaining popularity is inclusion, which involves having the child with an autism spectrum disorder (or other disability) attend a typical classroom for the majority if not the entire school day. Most children require the support of a 1:1 aide to be successful in an included setting. A smaller group of children are able to attend these classes without any additional staffing. The decision to provide an aide should be regularly revisited, as some children "outgrow" the need for such support. It is often necessary to adapt the typical classroom and portions of the curriculum to some extent in order to promote the greatest progress (e.g., increasing the amount of structure in the school day, setting up opportunities for peer interactions, providing visual cues, and other environmental prompts). Some specialized programs are attended by a mix of both typically developing children and children with autism spectrum disorders. This arrangement provides intensive teaching coupled with the opportunity for the children with ASDs to view their fellow students as role models. As for the typically developing students, they benefit from the opportunity to learn that children with ASDs can be good friends and classmates. Also, children exposed to ASDs in this way are often more tolerant of differences in others.

Inclusion can be quite beneficial for children who have learned to focus on a classroom teacher, follow a classroom routine, gain academic skills, and watch and imitate others. Research has shown that typical peers can be effective role models for children with an autism spectrum disorder, particularly when it comes to social skills.

However, realize it is not *always* advantageous to promote inclusion for your child. Some children with ASDs will obtain little benefit from this type of arrangement and, in fact, may regress due to the regular education teacher's lack of specialized training as well as the decreased opportunities for 1:1 attention. Some parents are understandably excited about the idea of having their child included in a typical setting merely because the child is no longer in a special education class. However, sometimes a specialized setting is warranted in order to promote your child's overall progress.

It is not uncommon for children with ASDs who are included in regular education classes to require some additional support, such as attending a "resource room" to get additional instruction in certain subjects. Also, since communication is one of the areas most affected by an ASD, children are frequently provided speech/language therapy outside of the regular education setting.

What Criteria Should I Use to Choose the Best Learning Environment?

How do you determine which setting is best for your child? There are many factors that need to be considered when making this type of decision. The most important factors to consider include:

Age

Intensive home programming tends to be most successful for children under six years of age. The older your child is, the less likely a home program will be the best choice. As children with ASDs near school age, home programs become more limiting in that they provide less opportunity for these kids to interact with their typical peers and engage in group learning. Age also becomes a relevant factor when your child is an adolescent. For example, you may find that it is more beneficial to concentrate on functional vocational skills rather than academics and therefore his classroom placement should include this emphasis.

Diagnosis

Particular ASDs tend to lend themselves to certain educational settings, although, again, every child's placement and programming should be individualized. For example, if your child has been diagnosed with Asperger's disorder, PDD-NOS, or "high functioning autism," strategies such as inclusion or placement in less restrictive settings will likely be most effective. For your knowledge, special education law requires that a child be educated in the "least restrictive environment." That is, the selected classroom should not be more exclusionary or intensive than the child needs. Therefore, a child with Asperger's disorder may be able to learn successfully in a "less restrictive" class (e.g., in a classroom for children with learning disabilities rather than one for children with ASDs). If your child has been diagnosed with childhood disintegrative disorder, Rett's disorder, or "low to moderate functioning autism," it is more probable that an intensive classroom setting, such as one for children with ASDs or mental retardation, is most appropriate.

Even if your child is in a more restrictive or intensive classroom, it is often possible for him to be included, or mainstreamed, for nonacademic activities during the day such as music, gym, or art classes. However, keep in mind that these nonacademic classes can be especially challenging for some children with ASDs because of their unusual responses to sensory input (e.g., echoing sounds in the gym or music room, or being expected to touch and manipulate art materials that the child may find aversive).

Availability of Services

The hard reality is that not all communities have a wide range of successful programs for kids with ASDs that employ well-trained and experienced staff. Your decision about educational placement may be hindered by a lack of services in your area. You should be well aware, though, that you *cannot* be told by your local school district that appropriate education is not available for your child because of lack of funds. That is, if your child's IEP outlines a specific type of educational program, your local school district is obligated to provide it (even if that means your child will be the only student in the class!) They are legally responsible for coming up with the money and resources. Therefore, when developing your child's IEP, make sure it includes specific descriptions of the type of educational setting that is warranted and do not sign an IEP unless you are completely comfortable with its contents.

This is not meant to imply that obtaining an appropriate educational environment when it currently does not exist in your school district is an easy task. You may have to fight long and hard and even ask lawyers to become involved in a due process hearing, as described below. A valuable resource in this regard is *Negotiating the Special Education Maze: A Guide for Parents and Teachers*, 3rd ed. (Anderson, Chitwood, & Hayden, 1997), which provides step-by-step advice about how to obtain the most appropriate educational services for your child.

What can you do, as a parent, if the preferred educational setup is not presently available through your local school system or you disagree that the arrangement the school believes is sufficient meets the criteria outlined in your child's IEP? For instance, your child's IEP may denote that he should obtain "intensive ABA instruction" and the school district shows you a classroom that they believe provides this type of intervention. However, upon observation of the class, you feel strongly that the setting does *not* provide intensive ABA instruction. Instead of fighting the school system when these disagreements occur, some parents respond to this situation by developing an educational program within their own home, such as a home-based ABA program.

Although this can be a highly successful route, it can be very demanding on parents, as they are usually strapped with the responsibility of finding funding, instructors, consultants, and teaching materials. The burden can be lessened somewhat if the school system is sufficiently astute as to provide support and guidance in the development of a home program. Sometimes school districts will agree to pay for the operation of these home-based programs, or they refuse on the grounds that they believe their own educational placement of choice is adequate and therefore a home-program is not warranted. If you choose to implement a home-based ABA program, another book in the "Topics in Autism" series, *Right From the Start: Behavioral Intervention for Young Children with Autism* (Harris & Weiss, 1998), describes what a home-based ABA program is and how it can function for your child.

Another option is challenging the school system for appropriate services for your child by initiating a due process hearing. In this scenario, an objective third party (a "hearing officer" who has extensive background in special education law) evaluates your child's educational needs and determines if the school system is currently meeting these needs or must create a new program to meet these needs. Various individuals may testify during a due process hearing, expressing their beliefs about what the child's educational needs are and how they can best be met.

If the hearing officer agrees with the parents' contention that their child is not receiving what he's entitled to, then the school system must allocate funding to develop or seek out appropriate services. The school can do this by developing a new program that incorporates the required educational methods either within the school system or in the child's home. Or the school may opt to pay for an already-existing, appropriate educational program that is outside the child's school district but already up and running. If the out-of-district program is well run and has an acceptable track record, this may be a more viable path than creating a brand new program. It is important for parents to gather information about available programs in their local and surrounding communities in order to make knowledgeable decisions in this regard. This can be accomplished by visiting various classrooms, talking to parents whose

> Your local school district is obligated to provide the most suitable educational setting for your child. In other words, you *cannot* be told that appropriate education is not available for your child because of lack of funds.

children attend the classrooms, and discussing the options with professionals who are familiar with your child's specific needs. Believe it or not, parents have significant influence over decisions about their child's eventual educational placement, so *be an involved member of the team!*

Prioritized Goals

Your decision about where to place your child may be affected by your most immediate goals for your child. As mentioned earlier, areas you may place at the top of the list include addressing medical issues, behaviors that place your child or others in danger, sleep disturbances, and development of communication skills. Prioritizing your child's developmental goals will likely influence your decisions about appropriate educational placement. For example, if you feel that your child's behavioral challenges are the greatest obstacle to learning, then you may decide that an intensive, behavioral classroom for children with ASDs is the only place where these challenges can be addressed successfully. However, another parent may identify the top priority as improved social skills with peers and therefore a classroom setting that provides extensive opportunities to interact with other children is optimal. Keep in mind that as your child grows, your priorities will change, and consequently your feelings about what type of educational placement is best may change as well.

Changes Through the Years

All kids grow and learn, and those on the autism spectrum are no exception. Try not to be discouraged if you are told that your young child needs to attend a more restrictive classroom initially. This placement may not be required for his entire academic experience. Don't be surprised if your child requires a more intensive setting when he is young but is transferred to a less restrictive classroom as he acquires new skills and competencies. For example, early on, your child may be placed in a classroom specifically for children with ASDs, then gradually moved into regular education classes, and ultimately fully included into a typical classroom by fourth or fifth grade. Less frequently, a child may need to be transferred to a more restrictive setting because of challenging behaviors or a decreased learning curve. However, this occurrence is rare and more often than not children are able to attend less restrictive settings as they get older.

What Treatment Strategies Have Shown the Greatest Success?

Over the years, a wide variety of methods have been used to treat people with autism spectrum disorders. While some techniques have faded due to their lack of success, others have continued to be supported in the research and anecdotally by families and teachers.

Although it is natural and understandable for parents to desperately seek a "cure" or seemingly the most effective treatment for their child, it is important that parents remain as objective and wary as possible. Spending time involved in a less than effective (or perhaps potentially harmful) treatment route can only take away from your child's overall progress. When evaluating whether or not a given intervention makes sense for *your* child, try to gather as much information as possible before making a decision. Evaluate reports from other parents as well as scientific research when making a list of pros and cons of each technique you are considering. Research journals, the Internet, conference presentations, materials supplied by the professionals involved in your child's care, and advice from other parents are all valid and helpful resources in this regard.

First, let's review a strategy you ought to **avoid**: *Facilitated Communication*. In the late 1980's and early 1990's, Facilitated Communication gained popularity as a means of helping people with autism spectrum disorders communicate. The method involves a "facilitator," an adult holding the child's hand while he types out a message using a keyboard or alphabet board. It was hypothesized that the children needed the physical support of having their hand held in order to feel comfortable spelling out their innermost feelings and needs. Hundreds of research studies subsequently demonstrated that the facilitator was inadvertently influencing the child's responses (Mostert, 2001). Given that the validity of this method has been repeatedly disproved, along with the high incidence of bogus sexual abuse allegations that have been made by children via Facilitated Communication, it is highly recommended you avoid this strategy.

Applied Behavior Analysis

What are the characteristics of an effective treatment program for people with autism spectrum disorders? The methodology that has been proven again and again over the past thirty years to be a very effective means of teaching people with ASDs is *Applied Behavior Analysis*, or ABA. This strategy incorporates what we've discovered about behavior over years of scientific research about how behavior is learned. Generally speaking, the classrooms and programs that have shown the greatest degree of success have incorporated these principles into their intervention plan. As discussed below, ABA programs are based on many years of research studying how behavior is learned and how it can be changed. Describing all of the characteristics of an applied behavioral approach is beyond the scope of this book; however, there are other books within the "Topics in Autism" series, as well as other resources that provide comprehensive descriptions of this approach. The following is a summary of principles and techniques of Applied Behavior Analysis that promote success:

> **ABA is Data-based:** All treatment techniques should involve consistent and reliable data regarding the child's progress. These might include charts, graphs, etc., which depict how the child's behavior is changing (e.g., how skills are being learned and how challenging behaviors

are decreasing). There are many ways of collecting data such as tallying each and every time a child demonstrates a given behavior, or noting whether or not a child answered a question the first time asked each day. Regardless of the particular data system that is chosen, there are many advantages of a data-based treatment program. First, the teachers and parents can actually see how the child is progressing. Second, the data drives decisions about whether or not teaching methods should be modified so as to be made more effective. Third, data can help assure that all staff involved are consistent and implementing the treatment program as planned.

ABA Affords Repeated Opportunities for Learning: Most people with ASDs require many opportunities to acquire a given skill. As compared to children who are typically developing, children with ASDs usually exhibit an inability to recognize important characteristics of the environment, retain that information, and then use it during future situations. For example, as a child you probably learned that you needed to raise your hand in class after being instructed to do so a few times. In contrast, a child with an ASD may have difficulty understanding the relevant environmental characteristics that cue him to raise his hand (e.g., in school versus at home, or when he knows the answer versus when he does not, etc.). The child may also not understand the words, "Raise your hand" due to deficits in communication skills. Therefore, it is often necessary to teach by repeated trials so that a new skill becomes ingrained and the child has more opportunities to recognize when the skill is to be used.

ABA Addresses Generalization Issues: People with autism spectrum disorders tend to have difficulty generalizing newly acquired skills. "Generalization" refers to the ability to demonstrate a new skill in novel situations such as in various locations, with different people, or new materials. For example, a child with an ASD may learn to identify colors while seated at his desk in school but not be able to demonstrate the skill at home, with a substitute teacher, or with different teaching materials. Consequently, it is often necessary to deliberately implement methods that teach a child to generalize his new-found abilities and to collect data regarding how often this is occurring. For example, as soon as a child learns to recognize the color "red," teach him to identify many red items in the classroom and community, as well as when people other than his teacher make the request.

ABA Shapes Behavior Through Successive Approximations: A child with an ASD has the best opportunity to learn a task when it is broken down into its essential parts and taught step by step. "Successive approximations" means that you are gradually increasing your expectations each time you teach a skill and providing reinforcement for better attempts toward the overall goal, thereby slowly "shaping" a child's behavior.

ABA Uses Reinforcement: Whereas children who are typically developing usually find learning itself to be reinforcing, children with ASDs often require some type of formal reinforcement, or reward system to increase their motivation to learn. Traditional methods of reinforcement, such as praise, report cards, etc., tend to be ineffective. It is often necessary to develop creative reinforcers according to each child with autism's personal interests. These reinforcers are then provided when the child demonstrates appropriate behaviors and skill development. The key to using reinforcers successfully is identifying the specific rewards that a given child will put forth effort to obtain. For example, one child found pirates to be highly appealing and therefore worked very hard to "earn" the right to wear a pirate hat and eye patch. Another child loved string and would work long and hard to receive string to add to his collection. Of course, it is important to pair these more unusual reinforcers with praise or pats on the back so that the child eventually learns to find the more traditional rewards motivating as well.

ABA Enhances a Child's Motivation to Learn: As mentioned above, many children with autism spectrum disorders do not find learning inherently appealing. Recent research has shown that a technique called "errorless learning" can increase a student's motivation to respond during a teaching situation. In the past, traditional ABA instruction involved asking a child to demonstrate a new skill, waiting a bit, and then prompting the child to respond if he had not already done so. This type of interaction can be frustrating for the student because he often has no idea how to respond. The resulting frustration can make teaching sessions especially unpleasant and tiresome.

Recently, research has shown it is more effective to provide a prompt *immediately following* the request when teaching novel or difficult skills to children with ASDs. This technique, known as "errorless learning," allows the student to always respond correctly. Prompting, either verbal or physical, is faded as soon as possible until the child is responding independently. Teaching sessions should also include a high ratio of "easy" tasks, which the child has previously acquired, so he feels successful and does not become bored or frustrated. That is, each "trial" (i.e., a request followed by a response) may ask the child to perform either a brand new task or an already-known skill and the majority of trials should involve easy tasks. Using this mixed trial format, rather than the traditional style of repeating the same difficult request over and over again across a series of trials, the child is more apt to attend, as well as to feel successful and motivated.

The degree to which each of the above Applied Behavior Analysis principles are incorporated into a child's educational and treatment plan will vary depending on his individual needs. While a child with Asperger's disorder may not need the majority of these strategies, a child with moderate to severe autism or childhood disintegrative disorder will almost certainly require extensive and intensive use of these techniques. It is important for you to gauge your child's abilities when deciding how intensively his teachers and therapists need to integrate these strategies to promote the greatest degree of success. As a general rule, the less responsive your child is to more traditional instructional methods (e.g., as seen in a regular education classroom), the more likely ABA methodology should be incorporated into his treatment plan.

Discrete Trial Instruction

One method that has been highly popular within the Applied Behavior Analysis framework is Discrete Trial Instruction (DTI). This method involves repeated opportunities for the child with an ASD to practice a given skill, using all of the principles described above. The typical scenario involves a child sitting at a table across from a teacher who repeatedly requests that the child perform a particular task. For example, when teaching color identification, the teacher might say, "Touch the red block." This exchange is referred to as a "trial" and identifying color is the "targeted skill." A given teaching session may involve twenty trials or more, mixing requests for the child to demonstrate the targeted skill with easy, previously acquired tasks. The teacher collects data on the child's performance, such as the percentage of trials the child responds to correctly, or noting whether or not the child responds correctly with a new skill the first time asked each day. The data are then graphed to provide an overall representation of the child's progress. DTI is a long-proven method that has produced significant positive results for many people with ASDs over the years. Although the specific way in which DTI is implemented has changed somewhat over the years, the general framework continues to be helpful for most people with autism.

The research that has been conducted with children under six years old indicates that the optimal intensity of Discrete Trial Instruction is forty hours per week. Needless to say, this is a time-consuming endeavor for parents and children. However, the results can be highly gratifying. For older children, DTI can still be an effective teaching technique even though the number of hours engaged in DTI may not be as extensive (e.g., a teacher may teach the student via DTI for a total of two hours during the school day).

DTI vs. ABA

Many parents and professionals misunderstand the terms ABA and DTI, and, in fact, often use the terms interchangeably. For example, a parent may say, "I have a DTI home-program," when in fact the home program is an ABA program that happens to include the use of DTI as an instructional method. It should be reiterated that ABA refers to a *range* of strategies, all of which incorporate research-founded principles of how behavior is learned and changed. DTI is merely one instructional strategy beneath the umbrella of ABA methodologies.

Controversies Regarding ABA and Related Methods

Some have argued that Applied Behavior Analysis and related strategies can have negative effects on people with autism spectrum disorders. One objection is that the repeated requests (or trials) can be tiring, especially for young children. Another complaint is that this method can inadvertently cause children to become "little robots" waiting for someone to make a request instead of initiating communication themselves. The fear is that spontaneous responses and speech will be hindered because ABA methods are often so teacher-directed. Some people view these methods as negative because in the early days of ABA, aversive techniques were sometimes incorporated into the teaching session. In the 1960s, if a child responded incorrectly or displayed a maladaptive (undesirable) behavior, such as aggression or self-injury, he was punished. Aversive techniques sometimes included slapping a child's hand or knee, spraying a water mister onto a child's face, or even electric shock. Fortunately, none of these techniques are accepted today.

These days, professionals emphasize the need to implement ABA methods in a positive, proactive manner, rather than relying on punishments or an authoritative attitude. Greater attention to offering highly preferred reinforcers (effective rewards) and using errorless learning techniques has made these methods positive, fun, and confidence-building, rather than stressful for the student with an ASD. As for the complaint that DTI methodology turns students into "little robots," a well-developed program includes many opportunities for teaching the children how to spontaneously initiate an interaction with others rather than waiting for an instruction.

In addition to ABA, there are other strategies that have been increasingly successful in teaching people with autism spectrum disorders. These include:

Visual Cues

People with ASDs often learn more effectively if provided *visual cues*, rather than verbal input only. Typically a child is expected to learn by simply listening to a teacher or parent speaking; unfortunately, since children with ASDs often have difficulty understanding auditory input, lessons are frequently ineffective. We know now that children with ASDs tend to be more responsive to visual input and cues, such as pictures and picture schedules, sign language or other gestures, and Social Stories (see below). Your child's learning curve will be significantly increased if the majority of teaching opportunities include a visual component coupled with verbal directions. For more information on visual strategies, read *A Picture's Worth: PECS and Other Visual Communication Strategies in Autism* (Andy Bondy & Lori Frost, 2002).

Social Stories

The use of Social Stories, first developed by Carol Gray, for teaching children with ASDs has gained increasing popularity over the past several years. A Social Story is a personalized "storybook," written by a teacher or parent, that depicts a specific situation. The beauty of Social Stories is that you can write your own, tailored to the special needs of your child. They include words, symbols, or images that help a child better understand a certain scenario that he has difficulty negotiating. These stories are read to the child during down time as well as when the problem situation is anticipated. For example, if a child finds the sound of the fire drill unnerving, a Social Story read ahead of time can remind him that the sound is only temporary, that he will soon be leaving the building, and that earmuffs to muffle the sound are available in his desk. Compared to merely describing these factors verbally, reading a Social Story to the child provides both visual and verbal input, thus enhancing learning.

Another opportunity to use a Social Stories is in the case of a child who finds it highly disturbing when his parents drive home using an unfamiliar route. The child becomes very upset and tantrums as soon as the parent turns "the wrong way." Fortunately, this particular child is a skilled reader and can read his own Social Story as his parents drive him home. Each page of the story recounts positive self-talk such as, "It's okay if we go home a different way" and "I can look out the window and watch the cars." This helps him be more rational and flexible. Within a few days, the child is able to stay calm on the way home, no matter which route is taken.

TEACCH

First developed by Eric Schopler and Gary Mesibov in North Carolina, TEACCH (**T**reatment and **E**ducation of **A**utistic and Related **C**ommunication Handicapped **Ch**ildren) is a method of teaching that incorporates many of the principles of ABA, such as shaping, prompting, and reinforcing target behaviors. Less research oriented compared to ABA strategies, TEACCH focuses extensively on changing the environment in order to facilitate learning. One of the goals of TEACCH is to create a highly structured teaching environment that enables the student to clearly understand classroom expectations. Work stations, or cubbies, and certain areas of the room reserved for specified tasks are designated by visual boundaries. For additional support, posted signs define behavioral expectations. Picture or written schedules of daily activities allow the students to anticipate what will happen next and respond accordingly. The teachers often label or color code the work materials so the children can visually discriminate what tasks need to be done and in what order.

One of the hallmarks of the TEACCH program is an emphasis on modifying the environment to enhance learning, rather than expecting the students to adapt to *our* traditional way of thinking. A perfect example of this notion is TEACCH's emphasis on work stations. Rather than expecting children with ASDs to learn to sit in a traditional classroom setup of rows of chairs facing the teacher, the use of work stations takes into consideration these children's need for a minimally distracting learning environment.

Activity Schedules

Lynn McClannahan and Patricia Krantz of the Princeton Child Development Institute (PCDI) developed the strategy of using activity schedules to promote independent, or less prompt-dependent, action from children with ASDs (McClannahan & Krantz, 1999). This technique involves creating a visual sequence (either written or pictorial) that depicts what activities should be done in what order. These visual sequences, or activity schedules, might show step by step how to brush your teeth, go through the lunch line, complete an academic assignment, initiate social interactions, or engage in play activities. The sequence can be provided either in the form of a picture book or, for children with more advanced skills, in the form of a checklist. The child is taught to point to each item, perform the task, and then return to the booklet or list in order to determine what comes next. By providing the child with a means of performing necessary tasks or leisure activities independently, parents are no longer required to prompt the child to move from one activity to the next. In this way, the child's overall independence is enhanced. For more information, check out *Activity Schedules for Children with Autism: Teaching Independent Behavior* (McClannahan & Krantz, 1999).

Self-Regulation/Self-Management Techniques

Robert Koegel and his colleagues have conducted extensive research on teaching people with autism spectrum disorders to monitor their own behaviors (Koegel & Koegel, 1995). The self-regulation techniques they have developed involve teaching a child first to recognize the targeted behavior via role-play, and then to actually count the number of times the behavior occurs. This technique can be applied to having the child count desirable behaviors (e.g., each time he initiates an interaction with a peer) as well as undesirable, or maladaptive behaviors (e.g., each time he begins to demonstrate a self-stimulatory behavior). Since many people with ASDs have compulsive tendencies as well as a special interest in numbers, this technique can be a highly motivating and effective means of improving behavior. Usually, reinforcements are incorporated into this self-regulation system in that the child may receive a reward if he shows a targeted behavior a designated amount of times. In this way the child is rewarded for demonstrating appropriate behaviors.

Adjunct Services

A comprehensive review of "add-on" services such as speech and language, occupational, and physical therapies is beyond the scope of this book; however it should be noted that many children with ASDs benefit from these types of adjunct services. Considering that communication is an invariable area of concern with children with ASDs, speech and language therapy is frequently provided either by the school system, via private practitioners in clinics at the parents' initiation, or both. Some people feel that occupational therapy can help children respond more adaptively to sensory issues. However, the jury is still out regarding whether or not these methods have been proven scientifically to help children process sensory information more effectively. Occupational therapists can also be involved when developing handwriting and other fine motor programs. Finally, a small group of children with ASDs require the services of a physical therapist if they experience developmental delays in the areas of gross motor tasks (i.e., full body movements such as walking, running, and climbing).

Medication

To date, no medications have been found effective in "curing" autism spectrum disorders. However, various medications have proven helpful in increasing positive behaviors or decreasing undesirable, or maladaptive ones. Generally speaking, no one medication is prescribed for all children with different types of ASDs. Rather, specific drugs are prescribed for specific symptoms of ASD (e.g., hyperactivity, obsessive rituals, or inattention.)

Parents are often resistant to medicating their child, and this hesitancy is understandable. In the past, available medications were often highly sedating. Although a child's challenging behaviors would often decrease with medication, he was lethargic and learning was hindered. Parents often couldn't recognize their own children on these medications. More recently, medications have been developed to target specific neurotransmitters in the central nervous system, rather than affecting the entire system. This advancement decreases the possibility of lethargy or other side effects. Although not required or effective for everyone with an ASD, medications have occasionally been responsible for significant positive change.

Antidepressants

Of the medications available today, a class of antidepressants called Selective Serotonin Reuptake Inhibitors (SSRIs) are perhaps the most widely used by people with autism spectrum disorders. Serotonin is a chemical in the brain, called a "neurotransmitter," which is involved in the transmission of messages from nerve cell to nerve cell. SSRIs regulate the amount of Serotonin present so that information can be processed more effectively within the brain. SSRIs have been found effective in the treatment of ASDs. Many SSRI medications are also prescribed for people without ASDs. Examples of SSRIs include Prozac™, Paxil™, Luvox™, and Zoloft™. SSRIs can be quite effective in decreasing irritability, rituals, repetitive or self-stimulating behaviors, and inappropriate speech, such as repeating the same words over and over (McDougle, et al., 1996; DeLong, et al., 1998). Although relatively uncommon, some of the most frequently seen side effects are weight gain, drowsiness (especially initially), increased irritability, nausea, diarrhea, headaches, and sleep disturbances.

One eight-year-old girl with autistic disorder, who had a long history of physical aggression, irritability, and noncompliance, had little success with traditional behavioral treatment approaches. Although she tested within the average to high average range in intelligence, her behavior was so challenging she needed to be placed in a highly restrictive classroom with minimal contact with her typically developing peers. However, once she was prescribed the SSRI, Paxil™, her overall demeanor improved and the incidence of challenging behaviors decreased significantly. Her general mood was elevated and she appeared happier and more at ease. She is now able to attend a less restrictive classroom and is learning basic math and reading.

Another antidepressant medication occasionally prescribed for people with ASDs is Anafranil™ (Gordon, et al., 1993). This medication has long been used to successfully treat people with obsessive-compulsive disorder (OCD). Similar to SSRIs, Anafranil™ affects the chemicals in your brain that can affect mood and behavior. Anafranil™ can also reduce the amount and severity of ritualistic tendencies in people with ASDs. Although Anafranil™ can be effective in decreasing irritability and repetitive movements and speech, there is a risk of high blood pressure and tachicardia (rapid heartbeat), so parents need to keep an eye out for these possible side effects.

Psychostimulants

Psychostimulants enhance the brain's ability to focus. Common examples of psychostimulants include Ritalin™ and Concerta™, which have often been used for children with hyperactivity and can sometimes help especially active or distractible children with ASDs focus. These medications decrease activity levels, which in turn can promote learning. Unlike many other medications, psychostimulants tend to "kick in" quickly and their efficiency can be judged within a short period of time, rather than after a long period of trial and error or waiting for therapeutic blood levels to be achieved. Psychostimulants have the added appeal of being able to be given on an "as needed" basis. For example, many parents feel comfortable having their children take a psychostimulant on school days but not on weekends or during summer vacations. Parents should be aware that psychostimulants can at times increase agitation and irritability as well as decrease appetite and promote sleep disturbances.

Antipsychotic Medications

In the past, some of the older antipsychotics such as Haldol™ and Thorazine™ were used to address challenging behaviors exhibited by children with ASDs. Unfortunately, these medications often caused significant negative side effects such as lethargy and tardive dyskenesia (involuntary movements of muscles that can be irreversible).

One of the newest antipsychotic medications, which is sometimes prescribed for children with ASDs, is Risperdol™. Risperdol™ can be effective in decreasing aggression, irritability, self-injury, social withdrawal, ritualistic behaviors, and overactivity. Although relatively safe as compared to the more traditional antipsychotic medications, Risperdol™ can still cause certain side effects such as weight gain and sedation. Also, although rare, tardive dyskenesia can occur in children who are prescribed Risperdol™ (Zuddas, et al., 2000).

Anticonvulsants

Anticonvulsants such as Depakote™ and Tegretol™ have traditionally been used to treat seizures. However, anticonvulsants have recently been found to promote mood stabilization and some people with ASDs show improvements on these medications (Childs & Blair, 1997). Positive effects can include a decrease in agitation and rapid mood swings. Side effects that can occur include nausea, weight gain, drowsiness, and liver problems.

Pros and Cons of Medication

Research shows ASDs are linked to abnormalities in the central nervous system, (i.e., brain chemistry), so medications that address these differences are a viable treatment route to consider. However, the use of medications for children with ASDs should only be considered after a careful review of the possible options as well as potential side effects. Once a given medication is initiated, ongoing data should be collected in order to assess whether or not the medication is having any positive *or* negative side effects.

It should be emphasized that medications should never be the sole treatment strategy for children with ASDs. Drug therapy should always be consistently monitored by a doctor and accompanied by individualized and intensive behavioral interventions. If you are considering medication for your child, remember that many children with ASDs do not react in a typical fashion to medications and therefore it may take some time before you hit upon an effective medication regime. Be patient and document any changes you may observe in your child's behavior, moods, sleeping, or eating patterns so that the prescribing physician can tell if the medication is working or not.

Alternative Treatments

Diet Modifications

Recently, many parents have looked to diet modifications as a means to promote improvement in their children with autism. Many have put their children on a gluten and casein-free diet. First, a word of explanation: Both gluten and casein are proteins. While gluten is found in all wheat, rye, barley, and most oat products, casein is found in all dairy products. Some people have hypothesized that individuals with ASDs have difficulty breaking down these proteins into their natural derivatives (known as "peptides"). As a consequence, there are excessive amounts of a certain class of peptides, called opiods, in the brain. Some contend that abnormalities in the way in which the gastrointestinal tract filters foods allows large amounts of peptides to enter the blood stream and make their way to the brain. Foods such as wheat, milk, cereals, etc. can act like opiods and exaggerate autistic symptoms, some believe. Therefore, a growing number of parents have removed all casein and gluten products from their children's diet. Although there have been anecdotal descriptions of positive effects with this diet, to date there are no reliable research data that support the contention that a casein and gluten-free diet is beneficial to children with autism.

Vitamin Therapy

Some specialists in the field of autism believe that people with ASDs have deficiencies in certain vitamins and can therefore show improved development if prescribed "megavitamin" doses (e.g., high doses of certain vitamins, such as B6, or magnesium, or a combination of the two) (Rimland, 1987). This strategy has been long-standing with certain professionals, although definitive research supporting its effectiveness is still lacking. It is important to note that there can be negative side effects of this type of megavitamin regime, such as muscle weakness, nausea, and a weakened heart. If you decide to go this route as a treatment, make sure that your pediatrician monitors your child closely, especially for the possibility of dangerous side effects. For example, if your child appears to have difficulty walking or holding onto objects, or if his heartbeat appears to become slower or more rapid, consult a physician immediately.

Parents of newly diagnosed children with ASDs often feel hard pressed to find a "cure" as soon as possible, especially given the emphasis upon early intervention as a time when children are most receptive to treatment. As a consequence, they may be especially open to the idea of alternative treatments. However, although some of these alternative treatments may eventually prove effective, it is to your child's benefit to move cautiously and objectively when making decisions about intervention and become knowledgeable about each treatment's possible side effects and risks.

Concluding Remarks

Knowledge regarding autism spectrum disorders continues to grow such that new theories about cause and treatments are being developed on an ongoing basis. Whereas earlier theories blamed parents for their child's condition, more recent research shows that ASDs are clearly biologically based and parents are not to blame. It's important to recognize that autism spectrum disorders are diagnosed via the presence or absence of specific behaviors that are relatively clearly delineated. However, at times misdiagnoses can occur, resulting in confusion and frustration.

As a parent, you need to assert yourself as an integral part of the diagnostic team and must participate fully in the process of making decisions regarding your child's treatment. Fortunately, as reviewed in this book, various treatment strategies have proven quite effective in improving the skills and lives of children with autism spectrum disorders and their families.

Although definitive "cures" have yet to be discovered, the overall prognosis for children with ASDs is far more positive than once believed. Thankfully, gone are the days when autism was considered an untreatable condition and parents were told to "put their child away" in an institution. When provided intensive and closely monitored treatment programs, children with autism spectrum disorders are gaining new skills every day. Although your child's rate of learning may be slow at times, you have every reason to maintain hope for the future.

Having a child with an ASD can be confusing, frustrating, and challenging. The usual supports that most parents rely on, such as advice from relatives or friends, parenting books, or memories of their own upbringing, are not always helpful when it comes to parenting a child with an ASD. Luckily, over the past ten years there has been a surge of interest in autism spectrum disorders. This has led to an increased understanding of why children with ASDs behave the way they do and how we can best help them lead fulfilling lives.

At the same time that the number of professionals specializing in this field has grown, parents have become more savvy about their children's needs. Many parent support groups have sprung up across the country that provide an opportunity to share ideas, advice, information, emotionally support one another, and just vent. Parents have learned how to be active and successful advocates for their children to assure that everything possible is being done to promote progress. As new strategies and research data come to light, professionals and parents working together will enhance the lives of all children with autism spectrum disorders.

Parents Speak

Trying to find the "right" interventions is an ongoing battle with many frustrations. We've listened to everyone's suggestions about how to treat our daughter. We've tried many options and have had to weed out what works and what doesn't. This is a very time-consuming process and there's no way around it.

࿐

We have dealt with numerous professionals in different disciplines in order to help Juan. We have stuck with those who have been helpful and stopped services with those that were not. Even though we are grateful to be able to utilize them, as parents, it can be so exhausting to be dealing with all of these professionals. We try to work as a team for Juan, as this is most beneficial for him.

࿐

Access to the Internet is amazingly helpful. Through it I've learned about special diets, auditory integration therapy, supplements, and support networks of parents all over the world who are dealing with this type of situation. We are not sure if what we've tried has helped, but as parents, we know we have to try *everything* for our peace of mind.

࿐

Her behavior at home has improved. However, school is another issue. Finding the right teacher is the key. If the teacher can adapt to the child's needs and idiosyncrasies, then school will be a more positive experience. We have to reassess where Jenny is each day and new suggestions and interventions are applied as needed. If the teacher is unwilling to adapt, then school is a negative experience and becomes a battlefield.

༺࿐༻

I remember the day Danny slapped his eight-year-old sister across the face. He had never hit her before. She cried and kept saying, "I didn't do anything!" Danny's behavior had escalated to an alarming point and I knew he needed hospitalization, but my husband hated the idea. The day Danny left for the hospital, my husband was so upset, he couldn't even say good-bye. He just kept fiddling with the clothes in his closet while huge tears ran down his face. That hospitalization was life-changing. Danny started medication for the first time. To this day (seven years later), we have never seen another violent outburst. My husband realized that sometimes we can't manage it all by ourselves and that asking for help, no matter how difficult, can be a blessing.

༺࿐༻

"If you are good in church, we'll go to the pool." We went to the pool every Sunday for five years. Curtis now sits through church and doesn't need the pool as a reward. Sometimes it just takes long-term dedication to work through a behavior problem.

༺࿐༻

Restraining our teenaged son is just not an option in our household. So, we've focused on behavior and functioning in the community instead of academics. It's great to have a child who is brilliant, but if that child doesn't use socially acceptable behaviors, it doesn't matter how smart he is. Our son is older now and can function in any social setting without behavior problems. He has enjoyed academic and social opportunities because of his terrific behavior. I have no regrets about putting behavior first.

〰

We resisted medication until our son was about nine. The options were not particularly attractive; the side effects horrible. Together, my son's doctor and I decided to think outside the "medication box." Six years later, the combination of medications we agreed on is still working and has never been increased.

〰

It takes a special team working together (i.e. parents, family, teachers, wrap-around providers, psychologists, psychiatrists, and therapists) to help make our child a success. There are many periods of frustration, but with each frustration, something new is identified and new options are then explored. The therapy has not been easy, but seeing my child happy and becoming more successful on a daily basis is worth all of the past frustrations. She really has progressed and it's nice to hear comments from other people who don't even realize she has a disability.

〰

Curtis was in an inclusive setting in his elementary school. One day he was very unhappy, screaming loudly. One little girl commented, "Oh, that's Curtis, he can't talk. It's okay, he'll stop when he isn't mad anymore." The environment of understanding and compassion in that school setting has followed Curtis to high school. If he acts differently now, the kids don't stop and stare. They know Curtis processes and communicates differently. Kids always say "hi" to him. They know he might not say "hi" back, but they still make sure to greet him daily.

Resource Guide

Autism Spectrum Disorders

Asperger Syndrome Coalition of the United States
P.O. Box 351268
Jacksonville, FL 32235-1268
866-4-ASPRGR
www.asperger.org
A national nonprofit organization committed to providing up-to-date and comprehensive information on Asperger's syndrome and related conditions. Offers articles as well as contact information for support groups that serve people with AS and related conditions and their families.

Autism Society Canada
P.O. Box 635
Fredericton, New Brunswick
Canada E3B 5B4
506-363-8815
www.autismsocietycanada.ca
A national nonprofit organization committed to advocacy, public education, information, and referral. Provides links to provincial autism societies and information related to Canadians with autism.

Autism Society of America (ASA)
7910 Woodmont Ave., Ste. 300
Bethesda, MD 20814

301-657-0881; 800-328-8476

www.autism-society.org

A national organization of parents and professionals that promotes a better understanding of autism, encourages the development of services, supports autism-related research, and advocates on behalf of people with autism and their families. Has a national network of local chapters and acts as an information clearinghouse.

Cure Autism Now (CAN)

5455 Wilshire Blvd., Ste. 715

Los Angeles, CA 90036-4234

888-8AUTISM; 323-549-0500

www.canfoundation.org; www.cureautismnow.org

A nonprofit organization dedicated to funding and promoting research with direct clinical implications for the treatment and cure of autism. Website includes links to information on ongoing clinical studies, research abstracts, news related to autism, and books and products.

Families for Early Autism Treatment (FEAT)

P.O. Box 255722

Sacramento, California, 95865-5722

916-843-1536

www.feat.org

A nonprofit network of organizations, sometimes called "Families for Effective Autism Treatment," devoted to advocacy, education, and support of families and professionals. It has many state and local branches; links to them can be found on their website.

International Rett Syndrome Association (IRSA)

9121 Piscataway Rd.

Clinton, MD 20735

800-818-RETT; 301-856-3334

www.rettsyndrome.org

The national organization for families affected by Rett's syndrome. Provides information, referrals, encourages public awareness of the condition, and supports research.

National Alliance for Autism Research (NAAR)
99 Wall St., Research Park
Princeton, NJ 08540
888-777-NAAR (6227)
www.naar.org
A national organization that works to encourage and support research into effective treatment and, ultimately, a cure for autism and related PDDs. It is a nationwide alliance of families, researchers, and others concerned with autism united in their efforts to fund and accelerate autism research.

National Autistic Society (England)
393 City Rd.
London EC1V 1NG
United Kingdom
+44 (0)20 7833 2299
www.nas.org.uk
The UK's foremost organization for people with autism and those who care about them. Organization can provide information on support groups for parents and siblings and "holiday facilities" specifically for young people with autism. Website offers information geared specifically to siblings as well as parents.

Online Asperger Syndrome Information & Support
www.aspergersyndrome.org
This website contains articles about specific issues (social skills, education, diagnosis, etc.) related to Asperger's disorder; links to products and other resources; message boards for parents, people with AS, and professionals; lists of private schools and camps, etc.

Yale Developmental Disabilities Clinic
Yale Child Study Center
230 South Frontage Road
P.O. Box 207900
New Haven, CT 06520-7900
http://info.med.yale.edu/chldstdy/autism
    Has information about ASDs and assessment, clinical and research programs, references, and many links to national and local autism resources.

Associated Disorders

The Arc
1010 Wayne Ave., Ste. 650
Silver Spring, MD 20910
301-565-3842
www.thearc.org
    A grassroots organization (formerly known as the Association for Retarded Citizens) that works to include all children and adults with cognitive and developmental disabilities in every community. Each state has its own office that provides services, including education, social, vocational training and support, and residential services. Website provides support and offers a wide variety of publications.

Epilepsy Foundation of America (EFA)
4351 Garden City Dr.
Landover, MD 20785-7223
800-332-1000
www.efa.org
    The national organization for individuals with seizure disorders and their families. Provides information and referrals, supports research, and promotes awareness.

LD OnLine
www.ldonline.org

A very comprehensive website that focuses on providing in-depth information about learning disabilities and AD/HD, but also has information of use to parents of children with any disability. Topics covered include assessment issues, special education, speech and language delays, social skills, processing disorders, nonverbal learning disorders, and more.

National Fragile X Foundation
P.O. Box 190488
San Francisco, CA 94119
800-688-8765; 925-938-9300
www.nfxf.org
Provides information and support to families of children with fragile X syndrome, promotes awareness of fragile X syndrome, and encourages research. Website includes a great deal of useful information.

NLDline
www.nldline.com
An online source of information about nonverbal learning disorders. The site offers many articles on educating, raising, and recognizing children with NLD, as well as other topics of interest such as bullying, executive function, and Asperger's disorder.

Other Useful Resources

American Occupational Therapy Association (AOTA)
4720 Montgomery Lane
P.O. Box 31220
Bethesda, MD 20824-1220
301-652-2682
www.aota.org
AOTA, the professional association for occupational therapists, has publications about occupational therapy and can refer you to an OT in your area.

American Speech-Language-Hearing Association (ASHA)
10801 Rockville Pike
Rockville, MD 20852
800-638-8255
www.asha.org
    ASHA, the professional organization for speech-language pathologists, has information on therapy and speech and language issues and can refer you to an SLP or audiologist in your area.

Behavior Analyst Certification Board (BACB)
519 E. Park Ave.
Tallahassee, FL 32301
www.bacb.com
    Website provides details about credentials necessary to be certified as a behavior analyst and the organization can assist in locating a behavioral consultant.

Disability Resources, Inc.
www.disabilityresources.org
    An extensive collection of links to information on many disabilities, including autism spectrum disorders, and to resources and support available in each state.

Family Village: A Global Community of Disability-Related Resources
Waisman Center
University of Wisconsin-Madison
1500 Highland Avenue
Madison, WI 53705-2280
www.familyvillage.wisc.edu
    This website has a great deal of information about disability and the family, autism, and other disabilities, as well as links to other sites, online support groups, listservs, etc.

National Information Center for Children and Youth with Disabilities (NICHCY)
P.O. Box 1492
Washington, DC 20013
800-695-0285
www.nichcy.org

An organization that can link parents to practically every government and nonprofit agency and organization involved in any way with disabilities. NICHCY's website provides extensive links and resources.

Sensory Integration International
P.O. Box 5339
Torrance, CA 90510-5339
310-787-8805
www.sensoryint.com

This organization conducts research into sensory integration dysfunction, provides training for therapists, and offers information and publications as well as referrals to therapists.

TASH
29 W. Susquehanna Avenue, Ste. 210
Baltimore, MD 21204
410-828-8274
www.tash.org

Formerly The Association for Persons with Severe Handicaps, this international organization advocates for and provides information about people with a wide range of disabilities, including autism. Publishes newsletters and journals.

Treatment and Education of Autistic and Related Communication Handicapped Children (TEACCH)
www.teacch.com

Provides information on the TEAACH program, and includes excellent sources of information, reading lists, organizations and support groups, and an introduction to autism.

Recommended Reading

Anderson, Johanna. *Sensory Motor Issues in Autism*. San Antonio, TX: The Psychological Corporation, 1999.

Anderson, Winifred, Stephen Chitwood, and Deidre Hayden. *Negotiating the Special Education Maze: A Guide for Parents and Teachers*, 3rd ed. Bethesda, MD: Woodbine House, 1997.

Attwood, Tony. *Asperger's Syndrome: A Guide for Parents and Professionals*. London, UK: Jessica Kingsley Publishers, 1998.

Baker, Bruce L., and Alan J. Brightman. *Steps to Independence: Teaching Everyday Skills to Children with Special Needs*, 4th ed. Baltimore, MD: Paul H. Brookes, 2004.

Baron-Cohen, Simon, and Patrick Bolton. *Autism: The Facts*. New York, NY: Oxford University Press, 1994.

Batshaw, Mark, ed. *Children with Disabilities*, 5th ed. Baltimore, MD: Paul H. Brookes, 2002.

Berkell Zager, Dianne E., ed. *Autism: Identification, Education and Treatment*, 2nd ed. Mahwah, NJ: Lawrence Erlbaum Associates, 1999.

Bondy, Andy, and Lori Frost. *A Picture's Worth: PECS and Other Visual Communication Strategies in Autism (Topics in Autism)*. Bethesda, MD: Woodbine House, 2002.

Brill, Marlene Targ. *Keys to Parenting the Child with Autism (Barron's Parenting Keys)*. Hauppauge, NY: Barron's Educational Series, 1994.

Callahan, Michael, and J. Bradley Garner. *Keys to the Workplace: Skills and Supports for People with Disabilities*. Baltimore, MD: Paul H. Brookes, 1997.

Charlton, James. *Nothing About Us without Us: Disability Oppression and Empowerment*, 2nd ed. Berkeley, CA: University of California Press, 2000.

Cohen, Donald J., and Fred R. Volkmar, eds. *Handbook of Autism and Pervasive Developmental Disorders,* 2nd ed. Hoboken, NJ: John Wiley & Sons, 1997.

Cohen, Shirley. *Targeting Autism: What We know, Don't Know, and Can Do to Help Young Children with Autism and Related Disorders*, 2nd ed. Berkeley, CA: University of California Press, 2002.

Coleman, Jeanine. *The Early Intervention Dictionary: A Multidisciplinary Guide to Terminology,* 2nd ed. Bethesda, MD: Woodbine House, 1999.

Condon, Gerald M., and Jeffery L. Condon. *Beyond the Grave: The Right Way and the Wrong Way of Leaving Money to Your Children (and Others)*. New York, NY: HarperBusiness, 2001.

Dillon, Kathleen. *Living with Autism: The Parents' Stories*. Boone, NC: Parkway Publishing, 1997.

Durand, V. Mark. *Sleep Better! A Guide to Improving Sleep for Children with Special Needs.* Baltimore, MD: Paul H. Brookes, 1998.

Featherstone, Helen. *A Difference in the Family: Living with a Disabled Child.* New York, NY: Penguin USA, 1981.

Fouse, Beth, and Maria Wheeler. *A Treasure Chest of Behavioral Strategies for Individuals with Autism.* Arlington, TX: Future Horizons, 1997.

Freeman, John, Eileen Vining, and Diana Pillas. *Seizures and Epilepsy in Childhood: A Guide for Parents*, 3rd ed. Baltimore, MD: Johns Hopkins University Press, 2003.

Freeman, Sabrina, and Lorelei Drake. *Teach Me Language: A Language Manual for Children with Autism, Asperger's Syndrome and Related Developmental Disorders.* Langley, BC: SKF Books, 1997.

Gerlach, Elizabeth K. *Autism Treatment Guide*, 3rd ed. Arlington, TX: Future Horizons, 2003.

Gerlach, Elizabeth K. *Just This Side of Normal: Glimpses Into Life with Autism.* Arlington, TX: Future Horizons, 1999.

Grandin, Temple, and Margaret Scariano. *Emergence: Labeled Autistic.* New York, NY: Warner Books, 1996.

Grandin, Temple. *Thinking in Pictures: And Other Reports from My Life with Autism.* New York, NY: Vintage, 1996.

Gray, Carol. *The New Social Story Book.* Arlington, TX: Future Horizons, 2000.

Gray, Carol. *What's Next?: Preparing the Student with Autism or Other Developmental Disabilities for Success in the Community.* Arlington, TX: Future Horizons, 1992.

Greenspan, Stanley, Serena Weider, and Robin Simon (contributor). *The Child with Special Needs: Encouraging Intellectual and Emotional Growth.* New York, NY: Perseus Books, 1998.

Hamilton, Lynn. *Facing Autism: Giving Parents Reasons for Hope and Guidance for Help.* Colorado Springs, CO: Waterbrook Press, 2000.

Harland, Kelly. *A Will of His Own: Reflections on Parenting a Child with Autism.* Bethesda, MD: Woodbine House, 2002.

Harris, Sandra L., and Mary Jane Weiss. *Right From the Start: Behavioral Intervention for Young Children with Autism (Topics in Autism).* Bethesda, MD: Woodbine House, 1998.

Harris, Sandra L., and Beth Glasberg. *Siblings of Children With Autism: A Guide for Families,* 2nd ed. *(Topics in Autism).* Bethesda, MD: Woodbine House, 2003.

Hart, Charles. *A Parent's Guide to Autism: Answers to the Most Common Questions.* New York, NY: Pocket Books, 1993.

Hodgdon, Linda. *Solving Behavior Problems in Autism: Improving Communication with Visual Strategies.* Troy, MI: QuirkRoberts, 1999.

Hodgdon, Linda. *Visual Strategies for Improving Communication: Volume 1: Practical Supports for School and Home.* Troy, MI: QuirkRoberts, 1995.

Holmes, David. *Autism Through the Lifespan: The Eden Model.* Bethesda, MD: Woodbine House, 1998.

Howlin, Patricia. *Children With Autism and Asperger Syndrome: A Guide for Practitioners and Carers.* Hoboken, NJ: John Wiley & Sons, 1999.

Kephart, Beth. *A Slant of Sun: One Child's Courage.* New York, NY: Quill, 1999.

Koegel, Robert, and Lynn Kern Koegel. *Teaching Children with Autism: Strategies for Initiating Positive Interactions and Improving Learning Opportunities.* Baltimore, MD: Paul H. Brookes, 1995.

Kranowitz, Carol Stock. *The Out-of-Sync Child: Recognizing and Coping with Sensory Integration Dysfunction.* New York, NY: Perigee, 1998.

Lears, Laurie. *Ian's Walk: A Story about Autism.* Morton Grove, IL: Albert Whitman & Co., 1998.

Lovett, Herbert, ed. *Learning to Listen: Positive Approaches and People with Difficult Behavior.* Baltimore, MD: Paul H. Brookes, 1996.

Marsh, Jayne D.B. *From the Heart: On Being the Mother of a Child with Special Needs.* Bethesda, MD: Woodbine House, 1994.

Maurice, Catherine, Stephen Luce, and Gina Green, eds. *Behavioral Intervention for Young Children with Autism: A Manual for Parents and Professionals.* Austin, TX: Pro-Ed, Inc., 1996.

Maurice, Catherine. *Let Me Hear Your Voice: A Family's Triumph over Autism.* New York, NY: Ballantine Books, 1994.

McClannahan, Lynn E., and Patricia J. Krantz. *Activity Schedules for Children with Autism: Teaching Independent Behavior (Topics in Autism).* Bethesda, MD: Woodbine House, 1999.

Meyer, Donald, and Patricia Vadasy (contributor). *Living with a Brother or Sister with Special Needs: A Book for Sibs,* 2nd ed. Seattle, WA: University of Washington Press, 1996.

Meyer, Donald, ed. *Uncommon Fathers: Reflections on Raising a Child with a Disability.* Bethesda, MD: Woodbine House, 1995.

Meyer, Donald, ed. *Views From Our Shoes: Growing Up with a Brother or Sister with Special Needs.* Bethesda, MD: Woodbine House, 1997.

Miller, Nancy, and Catherine Sammons. *Everybody's Different: Understanding and Changing Our Reactions to Disabilities.* Baltimore, MD: Paul H. Brookes, 1999.

Miller, Nancy. *Nobody's Perfect: Living and Growing with Children Who Have Special Needs.* Baltimore, MD: Paul H. Brookes, 1994.

Morgan, Hugh. *Adults with Autism: A Guide to Theory and Practice.* Cambridge, UK: Cambridge University Press, 1996.

Park, Clara Claiborne. *The Siege: The First Eight Years of an Autistic Child with an Epilogue, Fifteen Years Later.* New York, NY: Little Brown & Co., 1982.

Powers, Michael D. *Children with Autism: A Parents' Guide,* 2nd ed. Bethesda, MD: Woodbine House, 2000.

Quill, Kathleen Ann. *Teaching Children with Autism: Strategies to Enhance Communication and Socialization.* San Diego, CA: Singular Publishing, 1995.

Russell, L. Mark, Arnold Grant, Richard Fee, and Suzanne Joseph. *Planning for the Future: Providing a Meaningful Life for a Child with a Disability After Your Death,* 3rd ed. Evanston, IL: American Publishing Co., 1995.

Schlachter, Gail Ann, and R. David Weber. *Financial Aid for the Disabled and Their Families*, 2002-2004. San Carlos, CA: Reference Service Press, 2002.

Schopler, Eric, and Gary B. Mesibov, eds. *High Functioning Individuals with Autism*. New York, NY: Plenum Press, 1992.

Schopler, Eric, ed. *Parent Survival Manual: A Guide to Crisis Resolution in Autism and Related Developmental Disorders*. New York, NY: Plenum Press, 1995.

Shaw, Randy. *The Activist's Handbook: A Primer for the 1990s and Beyond*. Berkeley, CA: University of California Press, 1996.

Siegel, Bryna, Stuart Silverstein, and Glen R. Elliot. *What About Me? Growing Up with a Developmentally Disabled Sibling*. New York, NY: Perseus Books, 2001.

Siegel, Bryna. *The World of the Autistic Child: Understanding and Treating Autism Spectrum Disorders*. New York, NY: Oxford University Press, 1998.

Siegel, Lawrence. *The Complete IEP Guide: How to Advocate for Your Special Ed Child*, 2nd ed. Berkeley, CA: Nolo Press, 2001.

Smith, Marcia Datlow, Ronald G. Belcher, and Patricia D. Juhrs. *A Guide to Successful Employment for Individuals with Autism*. Baltimore, MD: Paul H. Brookes, 1995.

Thompson, Mary. *Andy and His Yellow Frisbee*. Bethesda, MD: Woodbine House, 1996.

Volkmar, Fred, and Lisa A. Wiesner. *Healthcare for Children on the Autism Spectrum*. Bethesda, MD: Woodbine House, 2004.

Waltz, Mitzi. *Autism Spectrum Disorders: Understanding the Diagnosis and Getting Help*, 2nd ed. Sebastopol, CA: O'Reilly & Assoc., Inc., 2002.

Waltz, Mitzi. *Pervasive Developmental Disorders: Diagnosis, Options, and Answers*. Arlington, TX: Future Horizons, 2003.

Wehman, Paul, and John Kregel. *More Than a Job: Securing Satisfying Careers for People with Disabilities*. Baltimore, MD: Paul H. Brookes, 1998.

Weiss, Mary Jane, and Sandra L. Harris. *Reaching Out, Joining In: Teaching Social Skills to Young Children with Autism (Topics in Autism)*. Bethesda, MD: Woodbine House, 2001.

Wheeler, Maria. *Toilet Training for Individuals with Autism and Related Disorders: A Comprehensive Guide for Parents and Teachers*. Arlington, TX: Future Horizons, 1998.

White, Burton L. *The First Three Years of Life*, Revised Edition. New York, NY: Fireside, 1995.

Willey, Liane. *Pretending to be Normal: Living with Asperger's Syndrome*. London, UK: Jessica Kingsley Publishers, 1999.

Williams, Donna. *Nobody Nowhere: The Extraordinary Autobiography of an Autistic*. New York, NY: Avon Books, 1994.

Williams, Donna. *Somebody Somewhere: Breaking Free from the World of Autism*. New York, NY: Crown Publishing Group, 1995.

Wing, Lorna. *The Autistic Spectrum: A Parents' Guide to Understanding and Helping Your Child*. Berkeley, CA: Ulysses Press, 2001.

Spanish Books

Anderson, Winifred, Stephen Chitwood, and Deidre Hayden. *Guiándose por la Intrincada Senda de la Educación Especial: Una Guía para Padres y Maestros*, 3rd ed. Bethesda, MD: Woodbine House, 1999.

Powers, Michael D., ed. *Niños Autistas: Guía para Padres, Terapeutas y Educadores*, 1st ed. Mexico: Trillas, 1999.

Magazines and Newsletters

The Advocate. The Autism Society of America, 7910 Woodmont Ave., Suite 300, Bethesda, MD 20814-3015.

Augmentative Communication News. Augmentative Communication, Inc., One Surf Way, #237, Monterey, CA 93940.

Autism Research Review International. Autism Research Institute, 4182 Adams Ave., San Diego, CA 92116.

Especially Grandparents. King County ARC, 2230 Eighth Ave., Seattle, WA 98121.

Exceptional Parent Magazine. 555 Kinderkamack Rd., Oradell, NJ 07649-1517.

Journal of Autism and Developmental Disorders. Plenum Publishers, 233 Spring St., New York, NY 10013-1578.

The MAAP. MAAP Services, Inc., P.O. Box 524, Crown Point, IN 46307.

Pacesetter Newsletter. Parent Advocacy Coalition for Educational Rights (PACER), 8161 Normandale Blvd., Minneapolis, MN 55437.

Positive Behavioral Change Bulletin. Positive Behavioral Support, University Affiliated Program, Rhode Island College, 600 Mount Pleasant Ave., Providence, RI 02908.

Sibling Information Network Newsletter. Sibling Information Network, 249 Glenbrook Rd., U-64, Storrs, CT 06269-2064.

References

American Psychiatric Association (1994). *Diagnostic and Statistical Manual of Mental Disorders (DSM-IV)*, 4th ed. Washington, DC: American Psychiatric Association.

Angelo, C. *For Our Children: A Lawyer's Guide to Insurance Coverage and a Parent's Call to Organize*. Available through the Autism Society of America (ASA), Bethesda, MD, 20814.

Baranek, G. (1999). Autism during infancy: A retrospective video analysis of sensory-motor and social behaviors at 9-12 months of age. *Journal of Autism and Developmental Disorders*, 29, 213-224.

Bauman, M. & Kemper, T. (1994). Neuroanatomic observations of the brain in autism. In M.L. Bauman & T.L. Kemper (Eds.), *The Neurology of Autism*. Baltimore, MD: Johns Hopkins United Press.

Bondy, A. & Frost, L. *A Picture's Worth: PECS and Other Visual Communication Strategies in Autism*. Bethesda, MD: Woodbine House, 2002.

Childs, J. & Blair, J. (1997). Valproic acid treatment of epilepsy in autistic twins. *Journal of Neuroscience Nursing*, 29, 244-248.

Courchesne, E., Carper, R. & Akshoomoff, N. (2003) Evidence of brain overgrowth in the first year of life in autism. *Journal of the American Medical Association*, 290, 337-344.

Courchesne, E., Yeung-Curchesne, R., Press, G., Hesselink, J. & Jernigan, T. (1988) Hypoplasia of cerebellar vermal lobules VI and VII in autism. *New England Journal of Medicine*, 318, 1349-1354.

Croen, J., Grether, J., Hoogstrate, J. & Selvin, S. (2002). The changing prevalence of autism in California. *Journal of Autism and Developmental Disorders*, 32, 207-216.

Dales, L., Hammer, S. & Smith, N. (2001) Time trends in autism and in MMR immunization in California. *Journal of the American Medical Association*, 9, 1183-1185.

DeLong, G., Teague, L. & McSwain, K. (1998). Effects of Fluoxetine treatment in young children with idiopathic autism. *Developmental Medicine and Child Neurology*, 40, 551-562.

Gillberg, C. & Coleman, M. *The Biology of the Autistic Syndromes*, 3rd ed. London, UK: Mac Keith Press, 2000.

Gordon, C., State, K., Nelson, J. Hamburger, S. & Rapoport, J. (1993) A double-blind comparison of Clomopramine, Desipramine and placebo in the treatment of autistic disorder. *Archives of General Psychiatry*, 50, 441-447.

Gray, Carol (Ed.) *My Social Stories Book*. London, UK: Jessica Kingsley Publishing, 2002.

Harris, S. L. & Weiss, M.J. *Right from the Start: Behavioral Interventions for Young Children with Autism: A Guide for Parents and Professionals*. Bethesda, MD: Woodbine House, 1998.

Koegel, R.L. & Koegel, L.K., *Teaching Children with Autism*. Baltimore, MD: Paul H. Brookes, 1995.

Lovaas, O.I. & Simmons, J.Q. (1969) Manipulation of self-destruction in three retarded children. *Journal of Applied Behavior Analysis*, 2, 143-157.

Maurice, Catherine (Ed.) *Behavioral Intervention for Young Children with Autism*. Austin, TX: Pro-Ed, Inc., 1996.

McClannahan, L. & Krantz, P. *Activity Schedules for Young Children with Autism: Teaching Independent Behavior*. Bethesda, MD: Woodbine House, 1999.

McDougle, C., Naylor, S., Cohen, D., Volkmar, F., Heninger, G. & Price, L. (1996) A double-blind, placebo-controlled study of fluvoxamine in adults with autistic disorder. *Archives of General Psychiatry*, 53, 1001-1008.

Mostert, M. (2001). Facilitated communication since 1995: A review of published studies. *Journal of Autism and Developmental Disorders*, 31, 287-314.

Osterling, J. & Dawson, G. (1994) Early recognition of children with autism: A study of first birthday home videotapes. *Journal of Autism and Developmental Disorders*, 24, 247-257.

Rimland, B. *Infantile Autism: The Syndrome and Its Implications for a Neural Theory of Behavior*. Upper Saddle River, NJ: Prentice Hall Publishers, 1964.

Rimland, B. Megavitamin B6 and magnesium in the treatment of autistic children and adults. In Schopler, E. & G. Mesibov, (Eds.), *Neurobiological Issues in Autism* (pp. 390-405). New York, NY: Plenum Press, 1987.

Sparks, B., Friedman, S., Shaw, D., Aylward, E., Echelard, D., Artru, A., Maravilla, K., Giedd, J., Munson, J., Dawson, G. & Dager, S. (2002) Brain structural abnormalities in young children with autism spectrum disorders. *Neurology*, 59, 184-192.

Wakefield, D. R. (1998). Autism, inflammatory bowel disease, and MMR vaccine. *Lancet*, 351, 1355.

Webb, T. & Latif, F. (2001). Rett syndrome and the MeCP2 gene. *Journal of Medical Genetics*, 38, 217-223.

Wing, L., Yeates, W., Brierly, L. & Gould, J. (1976). The prevalence of early childhood autism: Comparison of administrative and epidemiological studies. *Psychological Medicine*, 6, 89-100.

Yeung-Courchesne, R. & Courchesne, E. (1997) From impasse to insight in autism research: From behavioral symptoms to biological explanations. *Development & Psychopathology*, 9, 389-419.

Zudas, A., Di Martino, A., Muglia, P. & Cianchetti, C. (2000). Long term risperdone for pervasive developmental disorder: Efficacy, tolerability and discontinuation. *Journal of Child and Adolescent Psychopharmacology*, 10, 79-90.

Index

About the Author

Carolyn T. Bruey, Psy.D., is a Managing Partner of Developmental Disabilities Resources in Lititz, Pennsylvania, which provides therapeutic and diagnostic services to children and adults with ASDs. She is the author or co-author of chapters in several books, including *CHILDREN WITH AUTISM : A PARENTS' GUIDE* (Woodbine House, 2000).